# Understanding Diversity Through Novels and Picture Books

# Understanding Diversity Through Novels and Picture Books

Liz Knowles, Ed.D., and Martha Smith

**LIBRARIES**
UNLIMITED
A Member of the Greenwood Publishing Group

Westport, Connecticut • London

**Library of Congress Cataloging-in-Publication Data**

Knowles, Elizabeth, 1946–
   Understanding diversity through novels and picture books / Liz Knowles, Ed.D. and Martha Smith.
   p. cm.
   Includes bibliographical references and index.
   ISBN-13: 978–1–59158–440–7 (alk. paper)
   ISBN-10: 1–59158–440–X (alk. paper)
   1. Children's literature—Bibliography. 2. Multicultural education—United States—Bibliography.
  3. Middle school students—Books and reading. 4. Ethnic groups in literature—Bibliography.
  5. Minorities in literature—Bibliography. 6. Pluralism (Social sciences) in literature—Bibliography.
  I. Smith, Martha, 1946– II. Title.
  Z1037.K597 2007
  011.62—dc22  2006037728

British Library Cataloguing in Publication Data is available.

Library of Congress Catalog Card Number: 2006037728
ISBN: 978–1–59158–440–7

First published in 2007

Libraries Unlimited, 88 Post Road West, Westport, CT 06881
A Member of the Greenwood Publishing Group, Inc.
www.lu.com

Printed in the United States of America

The paper used in this book complies with the Permanent Paper Standard issued by the National Information Standards Organization (Z39.48–1984).

10  9  8  7  6  5  4  3  2  1

# Contents

# Chapter 1

# Introduction

Multicultural education celebrates the coexistence of many distinct cultures within a given context, such as a community or nation. In schools, we look closely at various cultures and create festivals featuring specialty foods, costumes, key words from the language, flags, maps of the country, famous people, and important products. We study the folktales, myths, and legends. However, with this kind of focus we miss a large part of our society by ignoring stories that will help individuals understand specific issues. Utilizing literature with an emphasis on realism helps young people to see how others are coping, surviving, and even thriving. This provides the opportunity for others to "walk in the shoes" of young people today.

A focus on diversity, rather than just multiculturalism, supports a much broader meaning and spans so many areas of our lives—political, social, in the workplace, in our community, in our schools, and in the way we treat each other. Knowledge and understanding of all aspects of diversity is of paramount importance in today's world.

"Diversity—the act of recognizing, appreciating, valuing, and utilizing the unique talents and contributions of all individuals regardless of differences or similarities relating to age, color, race, religion, gender, sexual orientation, culture, ethnicity, language, national origin, physical appearance, disability, marital, parental or family status, communication or management style, educational level or background, speed of learning or comprehension" (Magazine Publishers of America; http://www.magazines.org/diversity).

This very complete definition of diversity exemplifies many more important potential differences and similarities than the term multicultural. This book uses literature to define many aspects of diversity, focusing on personal experiences and situations. We look at realistic fiction and picture books to give us an inside look at how diversity issues affect our daily lives and how the issues are handled by various characters. Our criteria for selecting these titles is that by reading these stories, young people can live vicariously—dealing with issues real to themselves or to their friends, family, and community. They can see their lives validated through parallel stories and further understanding will help us to reject stereotypes.

The organization for the book is based on The Big 8 Cultural Identifiers created by the National Association of Independent Schools (http://www.nais.org):

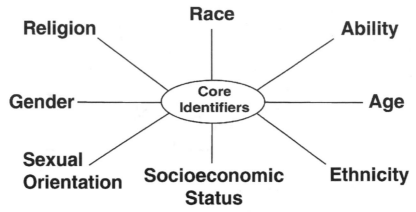

Courtesy of National Association of Independent Schools

We have chosen to expand the cultural identifiers of race and ethnicity to include the major ethnic groups:

Asian/Pacific Islander

Latino/Hispanic

African/Black

Native American/First Nation/Indigenous

Middle Eastern

White/European

Bi/Multiracial

In these sections we incorporated historical fiction titles to show the various conflicts, prejudices, and misunderstandings that developed in the past that have a direct effect on the treatment of the present-day people. In some cases the focus is only on historical fiction because there has not been much written in contemporary times.

We provide definitions (http://www.magazines.org/diversity) and discussion questions. We have selected titles ranging from picture books and beginning readers through general adult realistic fiction. The research is from the United States Census Bureau and the Gay Lesbian and Straight Education Network and we provide nonfiction, Internet, and magazine resources. We used Books in Print (http://www.booksinprint.com) for grade-level placement. We realize that this placement is arbitrary, and it is used to suggest the level for the books in the hope that all readers will find suitable reading material.

We also include annotated articles from a wide variety of professional journals:

*School Library Journal*  
*The College Board Review*  
*Book Links*  
*VOYA*  
*Teaching Tolerance*  
*The Social Studies*  
*Education Week*  

*Early Childhood Today*  
*Educational Leadership*  
*The Horn Book Magazine*  
*The Reading Teacher*  
*Kappa Delta Pi Record*  
*Diversity, Inc.*  
*Phi Delta Kappan*  

In the future, when our society becomes more blended, a book like this will not be needed because the lines of diversity will no longer exist. In the meantime, we hope that this book will provide insight and help to those who face the issues each day. We tried to select titles in which a character "lived the life" with the hope of promoting better understanding of all those with whom we come in contact in our daily lives.

# *Chapter* 2

# Research

In recent years, more than 1 million immigrants have been arriving in the United States annually. This has resulted in a country that is religiously, racially, and linguistically more diverse than ever before. Because of intermarriage, categorization of groups or identification of cultures has also become more difficult, according to the National Association of Social Workers (May 2005).[1]

The U.S. Census Bureau provides some amazing facts and projections about the diversity in the United States. According to the 2002 Census, 19 percent of the U.S. population over five years of age speaks a language other than English at home, and more than half of those speak Spanish.

In an article titled" "Nation's Population One-Third Minority" (May 2006),[2] the U.S. Census Bureau states that about one in every three U.S. residents is part of a group other than single-race non-Hispanic white. In 2005, the nation's minority population totaled 98 million, or 33 percent, of the country's total of 296.4 million. Hispanics continue to be the largest minority and fastest-growing group at 42.7 million. The second largest minority group was blacks (39.7 million), followed by Asians (14.4 million).

Another recent information bulletin published by the U.S. Census Bureau (March 2004), titled "Census Bureau Projects Tripling of Hispanic and Asian Populations in 50 Years; Non-Hispanic Whites May Drop to Half of Total Population,"[3] indicates that the nation's Hispanic and Asian populations would triple over the next half century, and non-Hispanic whites would represent about one-half of the total population by 2050. From 2000 to 2050, the non-Hispanic, white population would increase from 195.7 million to 210.3 million, an increase of 14.6 million or 7 percent. Nearly 67 million people of Hispanic origin (who may be of any race) would be added to the nation's population between 2000 and 2050. Their numbers are projected to grow from 35.6 million to 102.6 million, an increase of 188 percent. Their share of the nation's population would nearly double, from 12.6 percent to 24.4 percent.

The Asian population is projected to grow 213 percent, from 10.7 million to 33.4 million. Their share of the nation's population would double, from 3.8 percent to 8 percent. The black population is projected to rise from 35.8 million to 61.4 million in 2050, an increase of about 26 million or 71 percent. That would raise their share of the country's population from 12.7 percent to 14.6 percent.

In 2005, there were 36.8 million people aged sixty-five and older, accounting for 12 percent of the total population. The number of people aged eighty-five and older reached 5.1 million. The country's population is also expected to become older. Childbearing rates are expected to remain low, while baby boomers—people born between 1946 and 1964—begin to turn sixty-five in 2011. By 2030, about one in five people will be aged sixty-five or over.

There were 104 males for every one hundred females under eighteen in 2005. This ratio declines with age, however, to seventy-two men for every one hundred women sixty-five and older and forty-six men for every one hundred women aged eighty-five and older. The female population is projected to continue to outnumber the male population, going from a numerical difference of 5.3 million in 2000 (143.7 million females and 138.4 million males) to 6.9 million (213.4 million females and 206.5 million males) by mid-century.

Almost 13 percent of the U.S. population is below poverty level. Almost 21 percent of Americans report having at least one disability. In 2003, the U.S. Census reported that 4 percent of all married couples were interracial. In 2000, the U.S. Census reported that nearly 1.2 million gay people live with a same-sex partner.

Middle Easterners are one of the fastest-growing immigrant groups in America. Although the size of the overall immigrant population (legal and illegal) has tripled since 1970, the number of immigrants from the Middle East has grown more than sevenfold, from fewer than 200,000 in 1970 to nearly 1.5 million in 2000. It was last estimated that 150,000, or about 10 percent, of Middle Eastern immigrants are illegal aliens. Assuming no change in U.S. immigration policy, 1.1 million new immigrants (legal and illegal) from the Middle East are projected to settle in the United States by 2010, and the total Middle Eastern immigrant population will grow to about 2.5 million. These figures do not include the 570,000 U.S.-born children (under age eighteen) who have at least one parent born in the Middle East, a number expected to grow to 950,000 by 2010.

And finally, it is estimated that 51.2 million have some level of disability. They represent 18 percent of the population. Approximately 32.5 million people have a severe disability. They represent 12 percent of the population. Four million children (11 percent) aged six to fourteen have a disability, and 72 percent of people aged eighty and older have disabilities—the highest percentage of any age group. Among children under age fifteen, boys were more likely than girls to have a disability (11 percent vs. 6 percent); 10.7 million people aged six and older need personal assistance with one or more activities of daily living (such as taking a bath or shower) or instrumental activities of daily living (such as using the telephone). This group amounts to 4 percent of people in this age category.

Startling statistics about teens and sexual orientation are reported by the Gay, Lesbian and Straight Education Network (http://www.glsen.org). Homophobia is a major issue for gay and lesbian teens. Over 97 percent of students in public high schools report regularly hearing homophobic remarks from their peer and 53 percent claim they hear these remarks from school staff. It is estimated that 60 percent of public high school guidance counselors harbor negative feelings toward gay and lesbian students. As a result, it is estimated that more than 40 percent of those who have suffered physical attacks from their tormenters also attempt suicide.

In 1999, Susan Lempke stated in the *Horn Book Magazine* that despite the fact that the 1990s brought many immigrants to our country, the characters in our picture books did not reflect this change. Lempke shared statistics showing that of 216 picture books, 116 featured only white characters. And only 7 of the 216 picture books featured African American main characters.

Calvin Meyer and Elizabeth Rhoads (2006) wrote in the *Kappa Delta Pi Record* that we need to move away from the emphasis on food, festivals, folklore, and fashion in our study of cultures, which magnifies the differences. Instead, we need to teach understanding, respect, and similarities and work to transform existing attitudes.

Richard Kahlenberg, in the May 2006 issue of *Educational Leadership,* describes research showing that racial integration does not result in improved achievement in our schools. Socioeconomic integration, however, has a substantial impact on improving achievement for low socioeconomic students regardless of race.

And again in May 2006, Eileen Gale Kugler wrote in *Education Week* about the experiences of students in Annandale High School in Virginia. Students learned about the reasons immigrants are here, they learned differing points of view, and they watched immigrants work hard to achieve a better life for themselves and their families. Rather than focusing on the services immigrant children require, Kugler highlighted the positives that immigrant children bring to classrooms across the country.

Diversity is a topic that touches each and every one of us. We need to be aware that things are changing; to be conscientious citizens, we should value the diversity in our schools and communities. We cannot flourish simply by knowing a little about different cultures. If we want to help diverse students adjust and if we want to know more about the real issues they are facing, we need to provide them with realistic fiction and picture books, as well as some historical fiction and nonfiction, to heighten understanding and acceptance.

## Notes

1. Available at http://www.socialworkers.org/diversity. Accessed March 4, 2007.

2. Available at http://www.census.gov/Press-Release/www/releases/archives/population/006808. html. Accessed February 21, 2007.

3. Available at http://www.census.gov/Press-Release/www/releases/archives/population/001720. html. Accessed February 21, 2007.

# Chapter 3

# Authenticity

How can we be sure that we truly understand diversity through literature? It is imperative that authentic literature is grounded in accurate facts and information about the cultural identifier. Authors and illustrators must be true to the culture, and it is essential that they read extensively to make sure they portray cultural accuracy. Bishop (1994) states that some culturally authentic books are written by authors outside of the described culture. However, these are the exception rather than the rule. Those who were successful made a supreme effort to understand, learn, and inhabit another world in order to write about it. Misrepresentations are inexcusable and hurtful.

Norton (2005) states that authenticity is extremely important in nonfiction books and that facts about cultural identifiers must be accurate. It is equally important, however, for theme, setting, and characterization in fiction literature to support the culture, beliefs, and values. If we are going to use this literature as a type of bibliotherapy to help students who are part of the diversity issue as well as those who are on the outside just trying to understand the issues, then it must be based on accurate information. The story should be full of rich descriptions to help those who have not had the experiences and therefore it is imperative that the background is authentic. Brown and Stephens (1998) feel that it is also important to understand that several authors who are actually representative of the cultural identifier may see things from different perspectives. All authors should be immersed in the culture and extremely sensitive to the issues. Woodson (1998) relates that she is often asked how she feels about people writing stories outside of their own experiences. This angers her as she knows this question is only asked of authors of color—never white authors. She feels that the recent call for more diverse literature doesn't necessarily mean authentic (told by those who are) because there is a tendency to misrepresent. The author needs to go there and soul-search to get the exact experiences. She feels strongly, however, that all people should truly have the chance to tell their own stories. Nikola-Lisa (1998) claims that the inspiration she had for clarifying multicultural concerns is not from the personal relationships she has had but instead from some difficult situations from her past that needed to be resolved.

Campbell (1994) presents several arguments regarding the issue of whether the author must actually be part of the ethnic group to write a story successfully. The author must spend time in diligent research and immersion to produce an authentic work. The more obscure the culture, the more difficult a task this becomes. The call for more multicultural titles, the need to right wrongs, and the desire to be helpful to young people experiencing adverse effects from related issues are all good reasons for conscientious authors to try. Because we are greatly in need of quality fiction about the eight cultural identifiers, it is very important to make sure that any and all authors are diligent about their research.

# Chapter *4*

# African/Black

## Introduction

The Great Migration, the largest internal migration in our nation's history, began in 1910 and continued through about 1960. Approximately 6 million African Americans migrated from the agricultural South to the cities in the North and West. Immigration from Africa today is minuscule. In 1990, blacks constituted 12 percent of the population and were considered the largest of the minority groups. Today 750,000 Haitians reside in this country, one-third of whom live in Florida. Ft. Lauderdale, Florida, also has the fastest-growing population of Jamaicans outside of Jamaica. They number 70,000. With the 2000 census, Hispanics are now 12.5 percent of the population, and blacks are 12.3 percent of the American population. It is projected that this gap will continue to increase, favoring the Hispanics.

## Definition

**Black or African American:** A person having origins in any of the black racial groups of Africa. It includes people who indicate their race as "Black or African American," or as African American, Afro American, Kenyan, Nigerian, or Haitian. (Magazine Publishers of America)

# Annotations

Clements, Andrew. *The Jacket.* Simon and Schuster Books for Young Readers, 2002. ISBN 0-689-82595-1 Gr. 4–7

> Phil never thought he was prejudiced. He got along with the black students in school, but when he saw a boy ahead of him with this jacket, he grabbed him and accused the boy of stealing it. A teacher broke up the scuffle, and they were sent to the principal's office. It was there that Phil learned Daniel's grandmother was Lucy, who has cleaned Phil's home since he was very young. Phil's mother gave the jacket to Lucy for Daniel. This incident stays with Phil for days, and he is sensitive to what it must be like to be a black student. Phil is a good guy and tries to do what is right.

Crowe, Chris. *Mississippi Trial, 1955.* Dial Books for Young Readers, 2002. ISBN 0-14-250192-1 Gr. 6–8

> This is the fictional account of the murder of Emmett Till, a black teenager from Chicago. The story is told through the eyes of Hiram, who can't understand why his own father does not want to visit his family and hometown of Greenwood, Mississippi. Hiram is excited about going alone to visit his grandfather, but after participating in a racial confrontation, he begins to understand his father's thinking. Hiram attempts to share his leftover lunch with Emmett, when R.C. a local bully, forces Emmett to the ground. R.C. humiliates him by cutting open a fish and stuffing the innards into Emmett's mouth. Hiram is ashamed of himself because he stands by and lets it happen, while Emmett thinks Hiram is a friend despite their difference in color. Later Emmett is tortured and murdered for whistling at a white woman, but the thinking at the time among the whites in Mississippi is that he brought it on himself.

McKissack, Patricia C. *Abby Takes a Stand.* Viking, 2005. ISBN 0-670-06011-9 Juvenile

> Abby's with her grandmother in her attic, and they find an old menu from the 1960s. Thus begins the story of her grandmother when she was ten years old in Nashville, Tennessee. At that time, blacks and whites were separate. One day, when young Abby went downtown to the department store, she was given a coupon for a free ride on the merry-go-round. When she went up to the new restaurant, she did not see any signs saying Whites Only, so she stood in line for her turn. Not for long; she was told to leave because "we don't serve Negroes in here. Have you forgotten your place?" This prompts Abby to take a stand.

_____. *Goin' Someplace Special.* Simon & Schuster, 2001. ISBN 0-689-81885-8 Gr. PS–3

> In segregated Nashville in the early 1950s, 'Tricia Ann asks her grandmother if she can go someplace special. Her grandmother is not sure that she wants 'Tricia Ann to go off by herself but finally lets her go. On her walk through town, she is chased from a hotel lobby, then she is reminded that she cannot enter the movie theater through the front door and that once inside she must sit way up in the balcony. But she eventually gets to the place where she is welcome—that special someplace is the public library.

Myers, Walter Dean. *The Glory Field.* Scholastic, 1994. ISBN 0-590-45897-3 Gr. 7–9

> This is an in-depth look at the Lewis family, African Americans who continually struggle for freedom and equality. These stories show how each generation takes a stand against oppression and how slow and costly the process is.

Robinson, Sharon. *Promises to Keep: How Jackie Robinson Changed America.* Scholastic, 2004. ISBN 0-439-42592-1 Juvenile

    This photobiography of Jackie Robinson delineates his commitment to America and his challenge to all of us. Jackie Robinson helped break down racial segregation by being the first black man to play in the Major Baseball League. After a successful career in baseball, he retired in 1956 at thirty-seven years of age. In 1962, he was elected to the Baseball Hall of Fame. Jackie Robinson continued his commitment to America and received the nation's highest civilian award, the Presidential Medal of Freedom. In 1972, after he died, the Jackie Robinson Foundation was established to provide education and leadership development opportunities to young people with the expectation that they will give back to their communities. Jackie lived his philosophy: "A life is not important except for the impact it has on other lives."

Tillage, Leon Walter. *Leon's Story.* Farrar, Straus & Giroux, 1997. ISBN 0-374-34379-9 Gr. 3–7

    This is the story of Leon Walter Tillage as spoken on tape to Susan L. Roth. Leon currently works as a custodian at the Park School in Baltimore, Maryland, where he gives a speech about his life as a part of the curriculum. Leon was the son of a sharecropper and grew up in North Carolina in the 1940s. His life was about hard work and getting an education in an inferior school, about walking home from school, and about being passed by the white kids on the bus, who would holler and call names. When this happened, the black children would run and try to hide, but sometimes the bus stopped, and the white kids would get off and throw stones at whomever they could. Leon witnessed his father's being intentionally run over and killed by some drunken white teenagers, who were never punished for their actions. "In those days, Blacks didn't have any voice at all, and there was no such thing as taking the white man to court. You couldn't vote; you weren't even considered a citizen."

Woodson, Jacqueline. *The Other Side.* G. P. Putnam's Sons, 2001. ISBN 0-399-23116-1 Gr. K & up

    Two girls, one white and one black, are separated by a fence, and each keeps to her side. One day, Clover approaches the fence and meets Annie. They spend the summer getting to know each other while sitting on the fence.

# Bibliography

Beals, Melba Patillo. *Warriors Don't Cry: A Searing Memoir of the Battle to Integrate Little Rock's Central High.* Simon & Schuster, 1995. ISBN 0-6711-89900-7 Gr. 7 & up

Boles, Philana Marie. *Little Divas.* HarperTrade, 2006. ISBN 0-06-073299-7 Gr. 5–8

Curtis, Christopher Paul. *Bucking the Sarge.* Random House, 2004. ISBN 0-385-2307-7 Gr. 5–9

_____. *The Watsons Go to Birmingham—1963.* Sagebrush Education Resources, 2000. ISBN 0-613-85111-0 Gr. 5–8

Danticat, Edwidge. *Behind the Mountains.* Scholastic, 2004. ISBN 0-439-37300-X Gr. 5 & up

Draper, Sharon M. *Forged by Fire.* Book Wholesalers, 2002. ISBN 0-7587-0354-6 Gr. 7–10

_____. *Tears of a Tiger.* Thorndike Press, 2006. ISBN 0-7862-8361-0 Gr. 9 & up

English, Karen. *Francie.* Farrar, Straus & Giroux, 2002. ISBN 0-374-42459-5 Gr. 5–8

Flake, Sharon G. *Bang!* Hyperion Books for Children, 2005. ISBN 0-7868-1844-1 Gr. 8 & up

_____. *Money Hungry.* Hyperion Books, 2001. ISBN 0-7868-1503-5 Gr. 5–8.

Grimes, Nikki. *Bronx Masquerade.* Penguin Group, 2003. ISBN 0-14-250189-1 Gr. 8 & up

_____. *Jazmin's Notebook.* Book Wholesalers, 2002. ISBN 0-7587-0368-6 Gr. 6–10

Harrington, Janice N. *Going North.* Farrar, Straus & Giroux, 2004. ISBN 0-374-32681-9 Gr. 3-5

Hoffman, Mary. *The Color of Home.* Penguin Putnam, 2002. ISBN 0-8037-2841-7 Gr. 3–5

Houston, Julian. *New Boy.* Houghton Mifflin, 2005. ISBN 0-618-43253-1 Gr. 7–10

Johnson, Angela. *The First Part Last.* Simon & Schuster, 2003. ISBN 0-689-84922-2 Gr. 7 & up

_____. *The Other Side: Shorter Poems.* Scholastic, 2000. ISBN 0-531-07167-7 Gr. 5–7

Jones, Traci L. *Standing Against the Wind.* Farrar, Straus & Giroux, 2006. ISBN 0-374-37174-1 Juvenile

Jurmain, Suzanne. *The Forbidden Schoolhouse: The True and Dramatic Story of Prudence Crandell and Her Students.* Houghton Mifflin, 2005. ISBN 0-618-47302-5 Gr. 7–9

Kidd, Sue Monk. *The Secret Life of Bees.* Penguin Group, 2005. ISBN 0-14-303640-8 Young Adult

McDonald, Janet. *Brother Hood.* Thorndike Press, 2005. ISBN 0-7862-7334-8 Gr. 6–9

_____. *Twists and Turns, Vol. 5.* Thorndike Press, 2004. ISBN 0-7862-6664-3 Gr. 7 & up

McDonald, Joyce. *Devil on My Heels.* Random House, 2005. ISBN 0-440-23829-3 Gr. 6–9

McKissack, Frederick, and Patricia McKissack. *Miami Makes the Play.* Turtleback Books, 2004. ISBN 0-606-32802-5 Gr. 2–4

Miller, William. *Richard Wright and the Library Card.* Lee & Low, 1999. ISBN 1-880000-88-1 Gr. 4–6

Myers, Walter Dean. *Darnell Rock Reporting.* Yearling, 1994. ISBN 0-440-41157-2 Gr. 4–7

_____. *Handbook for Boys: A Novel.* HarperCollins, 2002. ISBN 0-06-029146-X Gr. 7 & up

_____. *Slam.* Scholastic, 1996. ISBN 0-590-48667-5 Gr. 8 & up

_____. *Street Love.* HarperTrade, 2006. ISBN 0-06-028080-8 Juvenile

Nolan, Han. *A Summer of Kings.* Harcourt Children's Books, 2006. ISBN 0-15-205108-2 Young Adult

Robinson, Sharon. *Safe at Home.* Scholastic, 2006. ISBN 0-439-67197-3 Juvenile

Rodman, Mary Ann. *Yankee Girl.* Farrar, Straus & Giroux, 2004. ISBN 0-374-38661-7 Gr. 4–8

Steptoe, Javaka. *In Daddy's Arms I Am Tall: African Americans Celebrating Fathers.* Lee & Low, 2001. ISBN 1-58430-016-7 Gr. 3 & up

Velasquez, Gloria. *Tyrone's Betrayal.* Arte Publico Press, 2006. ISBN 1-55885-465-7 Juvenile

Volponi, Paul. *Black and White.* Penguin Group, 2005. ISBN 0-670-06006-2 Gr. 9–12

Walvoord, Linda. *Rosetta, Rosetta, Sit by Me.* Marshall Cavendish, 2004. ISBN 0-7614-5171-4 Gr. 4–8

Williams, Lori Aurelia. *Broken China*. Simon & Schuster, 2006. ISBN 1-4169-1618-0 Gr. 8 & up

Williams-Garcia, Rita. *No Laughter Here*. HarperCollins, 2004. ISBN 0-688-16248-7 Gr. 5–8

Woods, Brenda. *Emako Blue*. Puffin, 2005. ISBN 0-14-240418-7 Gr. 7 & up

_____. *The Red Rose Box*. Sagebrush Education Resources, 2003. ISBN 0-613-87822-1 Gr. 4–6

Woodson, Jacqueline. *Behind You*. Penguin Group, 2004. ISBN 0-399-23988-X Gr. 8–10

_____. *The Dear One*. Penguin Group, 2004. ISBN 0-14-250190-5 Young Adult

_____. *If You Come Softly*. Puffin, 2006. ISBN 0-14-240601-5 Gr. 7 & up

_____. *Miracle's Boys*. Penguin Group, 2006. ISBN 0-14-240602-3 Gr. 6–10

_____. *Show Way*. Putnam, 2005. ISBN 0-399-23749-6 Gr. K–5

Wyeth, Sharon Dennis. *Orphea Proud*. Random House, 2006. ISBN 0-440-22706-2 Gr. 8 & up

## Picture Books

Birtha, Becky. *Grandma's Pride*. Albert Whitman, 2005. ISBN 0-8075-3028-X Gr. 2–4

Collier, Bryan. *Uptown*. Henry Holt, 2000. ISBN 0-8050-5721-8 Gr. K–3

Josse, Barbara. *Hot City*. Philomel, 2004. ISBN 0-399-23640-6 Gr. K–4

_____. *Stars in the Darkness*. Chronicle, 2001. ISBN 0-8118-2168-4 Gr. 1–3

Lester, Julius. *Let's Talk About Race*. HarperCollins, 2005. ISBN 0-06-028598-2 Gr. 1–5

Miller, William. *Night Golf*. Lee & Low, 2002. ISBN 1-58430-056-6 Gr. K–3

Pinkney, Sandra L. *Shades of Black: A Celebration of Our Children*. Scholastic, 2006. ISBN 0-439-80251-2 Juvenile

Rappaport, Doreen. *Martin's Big Words: The Life of Dr. Martin Luther King*. Hyperion, 2001. ISBN 0-7868-0714-8 Gr. PS–3

Robbins, Jacqui. *The New Girl … and Me*. Simon & Schuster, 2006. ISBN 0-689-86468-1 Gr. PS–2

Rosales, Melodye Benson. *Minnie Saves the Day: The Adventures of Minnie*. Little, Brown and Company, 2001. ISBN 0-316-75605-9 Gr. 2–4

Smith, Will. *Just the Two of Us*. Scholastic, 2001. ISBN 0-439-08792-9 Gr. PS–1

Tarpley, Natasha. *I Love My Hair!* Little, Brown and Company, 2001. ISBN 0-316-52375-5 Gr. PS–3

Weatherford, Carole Boston. *Dear Mr. Rosenwald*. Scholastic, 2006. ISBN 0-439-49522-9 Juvenile

_____. *Freedom on the Menu: The Greensboro Sit-Ins*. Dial, 2004. ISBN 0-8037-2860-3 Gr. K–4

_____. *Let Them Play!: The Story of the Cannon Street YMCA All Stars*. Dial, 2006. ISBN 0-8037-2987-1 Juvenile

Winthrop, Elizabeth. *Squashed in the Middle*. Henry Holt, 2005. ISBN 0-8050-6497-4 Gr. PS–2

Woodson, Jacqueline. *Our Gracie Aunt*. Hyperion Books, 2002. ISBN 0-7868-0620-6 Gr. 0–4

## Nonfiction

Adler, David A. *A Picture Book of Jackie Robinson.* Holiday House, 1994. ISBN 0-8234-1304-7 Gr. K–3

_____. *A Picture Book of Jesse Owens.* Holiday House, 1992. ISBN 0-8234-1066-8 Gr. K–3

_____. *A Picture Book of Rosa Parks.* Holiday House, 1993. ISBN 0-8234-1177-X Gr. K–3

Altman, Susan. *Extraordinary African-Americans from Colonial to Contemporary Times.* Children's Press, 2001. ISBN 0-516-22549-9 Gr. 6 & up

Bausum, Ann. *Freedom Riders: John Lewis and Jim Zwerg on the Front Lines of the Civil Rights Movement.* National Geographic, 2006. ISBN 0-7922-4173-8 Gr. 5–9

Bolden, Tonya. *Maritcha: A Nineteenth Century American Girl.* Abrams, 2005. ISBN 0-8109-5045-6 Gr. 0-4

Bridges, Ruby. *Through My Eyes.* Scholastic, 1999. ISBN 0-590-18923-9 Gr. 3–6

Burby, Liza N. *Jackie Joyner-Kersee.* Rosen, 1997. ISBN 0-8239-5064-6 Gr. 3-up

Coles, Robert. *The Story of Ruby Bridges.* Scholastic, 2004. ISBN 0-439-59844-3 Gr. K–3

Crowe, Chris. *Getting Away with Murder: The True Story of the Emmett Till Case.* Penguin Putnam, 2003. ISBN 0-8037-2804-2 Gr. 7 & up

Fradin, Dennis Brindell, and Judith Bloom Fradin. *Fight On! Mary Church Terrell's Battle for Integration.* Houghton Mifflin, 2003. ISBN 0-618-13349-6 Gr. 6–9

Freedman, Russell. *The Voice that Challenged a Nation: Marian Anderson and the Struggle for Equal Rights.* Houghton Mifflin, 2004. ISBN 0-618-15976-2 Gr. 5–9

Giovanni, Nikki. *Rosa.* Henry Holt, 2005. ISBN 0-8050-7106-7 Gr. 4–7

Haskins, James. *Rosa Parks, My Story.* Sagebrush Education Resources, 1999. ISBN 0-613-15120-8 Gr. 4–6

Igus, Toyomi. *I See the Rhythm.* Children's Book Press, 1998. ISBN 0-89239-151-0 Gr. 1 & up

King, Casey and Linda Barrett Osborne. *Oh, Freedom! Kids Talk About the Civil Rights Movement with the People Who Made It Happen.* Random House, 1997. ISBN 0-679-89005-X Gr. 9–11

McKissack, Frederick, and Patricia. *Ida B. Wells-Barnett: A Voice against Violence.* Enslow, 2001. ISBN 0-7660-1677-3 Gr. 4–6

McWhorter, Diane. *A Dream of Freedom: The Civil Rights Movement from 1954 to 1968.* Scholastic, 2004. ISBN 0-439-57678-4 Gr. 5–9

Medina, Tony. *DeShawn Days.* Lee & Low, 2001. ISBN 1-58430-022-1 Gr. 1–5

Miller, William. *Zora Hurston and the Chinaberry Tree.* Lee & Low, 1996. ISBN 1-880000-33-4 Gr. 4–6

Pinkney, Andrea Davis. *Let It Shine: Stories of Black Women Freedom Fighters.* Harcourt Children's Books, 2000. ISBN 0-15-201005-X Gr. PS–3

Porter, A. P. *Jump at de Sun: The Story of Zora Neal Hurston.* Lerner, 1992. ISBN 0-87614-546-2 Gr. 5–9

Press, Petra. *Coretta Scott King.* Heinemann Library, 2000. ISBN 1-575-72496-0 Gr. 4–7

Smith, Hope Anita. *The Way a Door Closes.* Henry Holt, 2003. ISBN 0-8050- 6477-X Gr. 5–8

Walter, Mildred Pitts. *Mississippi Challenge.* Turtleback Books, 1996. ISBN 0-606-09622-1 Gr. 7–12

Weatherford, Carole Boston. *A Negro League Scrapbook.* Boyds Mills, 2004. ISBN 1-59078-091-4 Gr. 4–6

## Series

*African-American Achievers.* Chelsea House.

*African American Biographies.* Enslow.

*African American Biography Library.* Enslow.

*African American Leaders.* Chelsea House.

*American Mosaic: African American Contributions.* Chelsea House.

*Black Americans of Achievement.* Chelsea House.

*Black Americans of Achievement, Legacy Edition.* Chelsea House.

*Fact Finders Biographies: Great African Americans.* Capstone Press.

# Discussion Questions

- Are the main characters in a setting other than urban inter city?
- Does the story line enhance a feeling of pride and connection with the portrayed minority?
- Does the story increase understanding and promote toleration and acceptance?
- Are the characters not stereotypical but true to life?

# Featured Authors

## Walter Dean Myers

**Birthplace:** Martinsburg, West Virginia
**Date of Birth:** August 12, 1937
**Current Home:** Jersey City, New Jersey
**Titles**

*Street Love* (2006)

*Harlem Hellfighters* (2005)

*Autobiography of My Dead Brother* (2005)

*Shooter* (2004)

*The Beast* (2003)

*Dream Bearer* (2003)

*I've Seen the Promised Land* (2003)

*It Ain't All for Nothin'* (2003)

*Crystal* (2002)

*Journal of Biddy Owens, the Negro Leagues* (2001)

*Patrol: An American Soldier in Vietnam* (2001)

*The Greatest: Muhammad Ali* (2001)

*Bad Boy: A Memoir* (2001)

*Blues of Flats Brown* (2000)

*145th Street: Short Stories* (2000)

*The Journal of Scott Pendleton Collins: A World War II Soldier* (1999)

*The Journal of Joshua Loper* (1999)

*At Her Majesty's Request* (1999)

*Monster* (1999)

*Angel to Angel* (1998)

*Amistad: A Long Road to Freedom* (1998)

*Harlem* (1997)

*How Mr. Monkey Saw the Whole World* (1996)

*One More River to Cross: An African American Photograph Album* (1996)

*Slam* (1996)

*Smiffy Blue: Ace Crime Detective: The Case of the Missing Ruby and Other Stories* (1996)

*Toussaint L'Ouverture* (1996)

*The Dragon Takes a Wife* (1995)

*Glorious Angels: An Album of Pictures and Verse* (1995)

*The Glory Field* (1995)

*Shadow of the Red Moon* (1995)

*The Story of the Three Kingdoms* (1995)

*Darnell Rock Reporting* (1994)

*Brown Angels: An Album of Pictures and Verse* (1993)

*Dangerous Games* (1993)

*Malcolm X: By Any Means Necessary* (1993)

*A Place Called Heartbreak: A Story of Vietnam* (1993)

*Young Martin's Promise* 1993)

*Mop, Moondance, and the Nagasaki Knights* (1992)

*The Righteous Revenge of Artemis Bonner* (1992)

*Somewhere in the Darkness* (1992)

*Now Is Your Time* (1991)

*The Mouse Rap* (1990)

*The Young Landlords* (1989)

*Fallen Angels* (1988)

*Fast Sam, Cool Clyde, and Stuff* (1988)

*Me, Mop, and the Moondance Kid* (1988)

*Scorpions* (1988)

*Crystal* (1987)

*Sweet Illusions* (1987)

*Ambush in the Amazon* (1986)

*Duel in the Desert* (1986)

*Adventure in Granada* (1985)

*The Hidden Shrine* (1985)

*The Outside Shot* (1984)

*Won't Know Till I Get There* (1982)

**Interesting Information**

- Myers's mother died when he was three, and his father gave him up for adoption.

- His adopted parents lived in Harlem, where he grew up.

- As a child, he had a speech impediment.

**Web Site:** http://www.walterdeanmyersbooks.com

**Contact:**
c/o HarperCollins
1350 Avenue of the Americas
New York, NY 10019

# Jacqueline Woodson

**Birthplace:** Columbus, Ohio
**Date of Birth:** February 12, 1963
**Current Home:** Brooklyn, New York
**Titles**

*Feathers* (2007)

*If You Come Softly* (2006)

*Show Way* (2005)

*Behind You* (2004)

*Coming on Home Soon* (2004)

*The House You Pass on the Way* (2003)

*Locomotion* (2003)

*Between Madison and Palmetto* (2002)

*Hush* (2002)

*Visiting Day* (2002)

*The Other Side* (2001)

*Miracle's Boys* (2000)

*Sweet, Sweet Memory* (2000)

*Lena* (1998)

*The House You Pass on the Way* (1997)

*From the Notebooks of Melanin Sun* (1995)

*The Dear One* (1991)

**Interesting Information**

- In fifth grade, Woodson edited her school's literary magazine.

- She does not believe in censorship.

- She writes about things that actually happen to kids that adults don't want to talk about.

**Web Site:** http://www.jacquelinewoodson.com

# Annotated Journal Articles

Tatum, Alfred W. "Engaging African Males in Reading." Educational Leadership. (February 2005): 44–48.

   The article suggests that when African American males demonstrate cultural-specific coping mechanism at school these behaviors result in suspensions and retentions because they are misinterpreted. There is a serious scarcity of good role models and an overabundance of negative role models for today's African American male adolescents. The author suggests that specific literacy programs must be culturally responsive to help these adolescent males. The author includes a list of recommended titles and a detailed description of the types of programs needed.

Taylor, Deborah. "Jacqueline Woodson." *School Library Journal.* (June 2006): 42–45.

   In January, 2006, Jacqueline Woodson received the prestigious Margaret A. Edwards Award from the Young Adult Library Services Association, part of the American Library Association. The award honors authors for lifetime contributions to young peoples' literature. Since her first title appeared in 1990, Ms. Woodson has addressed the most difficult social issues: poverty, prejudice, and violence. In an interview with Ms. Woodson, she shares insights on her childhood, her writing, and her feelings about her topics and her teen readers.

# Resources

## Books

*African American Biography.* 4 vols. UXL, 1993. ISBN 0-8103-9234-8 Middle School

*African American Culture and History: A Student's Guide.* 4 vols. Macmillan, 2000. ISBN 0-02-865531-1 Gr. 6-up

Hudson, Wade. *Afro-Bets Book of Black Heroes from A to Z: An Introduction to Important Black Achievers for Young Readers.* Just Us Books, 1998. ISBN 0-940-97502-5

*Student Almanac of African American History.* 2 vols. Greenwood, 2003. ISBN 0-313-32596-0 Middle School

## Organizations

Congressional Black Caucus Foundation
National Black Child Development Institute
1101 15th St NW, 900
Washington, D.C. 20005
http://www.nbcdi.org/Welcome

National Association for the Advancement of Colored People
4805 Mt. Hope Drive
Baltimore, MD 21215
1 (877) NAACP 98
info@naacp.org

## Web Sites

**The African-American Mosaic Exhibition (Library of Congress):** http://www.loc.gov/exhibits. african.into

**Civilrights.org:** www.civilrights.org

**KODAK: Powerful Days in Black and White:** http://www.kodak.com/US/en/corp/features/ moore.moorIndex

# Awards

## Coretta Scott King Awards

The origin of this award goes back to the late 1960s and continued on until 1982 when the American Library Association recognized it as an association award. Today the award is given to an African American author and an African American illustrator for exceptional books that "promote understanding and appreciation of the culture of all peoples and their contribution to the realization of the American dream"

(American Library Association). Web site: http://www.ala.org/ala/emiert/corettascottkingbookawards/ corettascott.htm

### 2005 Winners and Honor Books

**Coretta Scott King Author Award**

Morrison, Toni. *Remember: The Journey to School Integration.*

Moses, Sheila P. *The Legend of Buddy Bush.*

Flake, Sharon G. *Who Am I Without Him?: Short Stories about Girls and the Boys in Their Lives.*

Nelson, Marilyn. *Fortune's Bones: The Manumission Requiem.*

**Coretta Scott King Illustrator Award**

Kadir, A. Nelson for *Ellington Was Not a Street,* written by Ntozake Shange.

Coretta Scott King Illustrator Honor Award

Hamilton, Virginia. *People Could Fly: The Picture Book,* written by Leo and Diane Dillon.

Pinkney, Jerry. *God Bless the Child,* written by Billie Holiday and Arthur Herzog, Jr.

## John Steptoe Award for New Talent

This award was established in 1995 and is given annually to a black author and black illustrator at the beginning of their career, for text or illustrations for an outstanding book. They may only receive the award once.

### 2005 Award Winners

**Author:** Barbara Hathaway for *Missy Violet and Me.*
**Illustrator:** Frank Morrison for *Jazzy Miz Mozetta,* written by Brenda C. Roberts

### 2004 Award Winners

**Author:** Hope Anita Smith for *The Way a Door Closes*, illustrated by Shane W. Evans
**Illustrator:** Elbrite Brown for *My Family Plays Music,* written by Judy Cox.

# Chapter 5

# Asians

## Introduction

Discrimination against Asians began as early as 1862, with the Chinese Exclusion Act, which excluded the Chinese from immigrating and denied naturalization and democratic rights to Asians living in the United States. Prior to this, the Chinese were allowed to go to the "Golden Mountain" just after gold was discovered in California.

During this same time, Japanese were immigrating to Hawaii, where they worked on the sugar plantations. In the early 1900s, President Theodore Roosevelt limited the number of Japanese laborers who could work in the United States. With the Immigration Act of 1924, there was a total ban on Japanese immigration until the McCarren-Walter Act in 1952. This act allowed only one hundred immigrants from each South and East Asia country per year. It also allowed non-white immigrants to become U.S. citizens.

The largest wave of Asian immigration began with the Immigration Act of 1965, which abolished national origin quotas and allowed 20,000 immigrants per country per year. Many of these Asians were students, professionals, refugees from Vietnam, Cambodia, and middle- and upper-class Asians seeking political asylum. Over the years, Asians have earned a reputation as being hardworking, intelligent, and academically successful. Not all Asians have these characteristics, but these feelings may be expressed in the literature.

## Definition

**Asian:** A person having origins in any of the original peoples of the Far East, Southeast Asia, or the Indian subcontinent including, for example, Cambodia, China, India, Japan, Korea, Malaysia, Pakistan, the Philippine Islands, Thailand, and Vietnam. It includes "Asian Indian," "Chinese," "Filipino," "Korean," "Japanese," "Vietnamese," and "Other Asian." (Magazine Publishers of America)

21

# Annotations

Kadohata, Cynthia. *Weedflower*. Atheneum Books for Young Readers, 2006. ISBN 0-689-04937-4 Gr. 5–8 Japanese

Sumiko is excited about going to a schoolmate's birthday party—it's the first birthday party she's ever attended. The whole class is invited. When she arrives, the shocked mother promptly uninvites her. Humiliated and lonely, Sumiko waits on the bench for her father to pick her up. Shortly after this, Pearl Harbor is bombed by the Japanese, and life for the local Nikkei, or ethnically Japanese, changes drastically. All leaders in the Japanese community are sent away first with very little notice. Then the families are ordered to sell their belongings and leave for the internment camps. Sumiko and her family, minus her grandfather and father, are sent to live in the desert near Poston, Arizona. Boredom sets in quickly, so Sumiko and her elderly neighbor set out to create the best possible garden. At first there were no boundaries to the camp, and Sumiko meets an Indian boy. She realizes that he, too, is angry at the Japanese, but in his case, it's because he believed they should not be on the reservation. The only benefit the Indians will have is that when the Japanese leave, they will leave behind water to irrigate the reservation. Slowly, Frank and Sumiko, or Weedflower as he likes to call her, discover that they have much in common and that they both need a friend.

Lin, Grace. *The Year of the Dog*. Little, Brown and Company, 2006. ISBN 0-316-06002-X Gr. 3–5 Taiwanese

Pacy is looking forward to a year of good luck, new friends, and discovering her talents during this Chinese Year of the Dog. However, Pacy is confused. Is she Chinese or Taiwanese? When she asks her parents, they say she is American. Sometimes Pacy feels like she is living in two worlds. One day a new student, Melody, arrives at school, and she is also Taiwanese. Pacy, or Grace as she is called in school, has a new best friend who looks like her, and together they share similar backgrounds and traditions. Grace wins a prize for a book she illustrates and writes about her mother's ugly Chinese vegetables, which she grows and blends together to make a wonderful soup. When the year is over, Pacy decides it was a great year: "it was the year that I found myself and decided I was going to make books when I grew up." The author based this book on her own life, and she wrote it because she wished she had a book like it when she grew up, a book with a character like her.

Look, Lenore. *Ruby Lu, Brave and True*. Simon & Schuster, 2006. ISBN 1-4169-1389-0 Gr. 1-3 Chinese

Ruby Lu lives on 20th Avenue South with her Chinese Mother and American-born Chinese father and her younger brother Oscar. Ruby Lu loves magic and wearing her many colorful capes that her mother has made for her. She performs Ruby's Magic Madness for all of her friends on the street. Every chapter may be read as a stand-alone story, but put it all together and you have *Ruby Lu, Brave and True* and her adventures.

Marsden, Carolyn. *The Quail Club*. Candlewick Press, 2006. ISBN 0-7636-2635-X Gr. 3–5 Thai

This is a sequel to the *Gold Threaded Dress*. Oy wants to participate in the school's talent show. She is torn between doing a traditional Thai dance or performing an American dance with a bossy Liliandra, who will throw her out of the Quail Club if she does not. Oy knows she could never perform an American dance in public, so she asks Liliandra if she would like to learn the Thai chicken dance. Both girls learn about each other's home life and culture.

McMahon, Patricia. *Just Add One Chinese Sister: An Adoption Story.* Boyds Mills, 2005. ISBN 1-56397-989-6 Gr. PK–4 Chinese

> A little boy wonders how he will become a brother. His family receives a picture of a sad little Chinese girl who they are going to adopt. The three of them travel to China, and when they pick up his new baby sister, Claire, whom they are ready to love, all she can do is cry. Mother knows that they can help her be anything she wants to be. When Claire finally laughs, it is as if a dam broke; from then on she laughs and laughs. In answer to his original question, how do you become a brother, *add just one Chinese sister.*

Park, Linda Sue. *Bee-bim Bop!* Clarion Books, 2005. ISBN 0-618-26511-2 Gr. PS–2 Korean

> A mother and a little girl prepare the ingredients for Bee-bim Bop. The verse and illustrations match as you see the hungry little girl get more excited the closer they are to finishing the popular Korean dish. *Bop* is rice, which is placed in your bowl, then you top it with vegetables and meat, which you *bee-bim* or mix-mix like crazy. The recipe for this delicious and colorful meal in included.

Perkins, Mitali. *The Not-So-Star-Spangled Life of Sunita Sen.* Little, Brown and Company, 1993. ISBN0-316-15512-8 Gr. 6–9 Asian Indian

> What is happening to Sunni? She thought she knew who she was until her grandparents from India come to America for the year. Her mother stops teaching at the University, stays home cooking and cleaning, and puts aside her jeans and now wears only a sari. Sunni is not allowed to have her boyfriend Michael over because her grandparents came, and she is too embarrassed to tell him that it is not the custom in India for a boy to visit his girlfriend at her home. Why doesn't she have a normal family? It will take most of the year for Sunita to realize that her mother is also having trouble trying to please her parents by being the ideal Indian daughter. Sunita takes matters into her own hands, helps her mother, and learns to value her Indian heritage when she understands that it is her differences that make her who she is.

Wong, Li Keng. *Good Fortune: My Journey to Gold Mountain.* Peachtree, 2006. ISBN 1-56145-367-6 Gr. 4–7 Chinese

> Angel Island in the San Francisco Bay area was the "Ellis Island" of the West. It is here that the author first experienced the United States or the "Gold Mountain." The Chinese were first accepted when there was a need for cheap labor but later were seen as a threat. Chinese men were not allowed to bring their wives and children at that time. Therefore, when the author was young and her father had saved his money and brought her mother and three children to the United States, they had to say it was their aunt who was accompanying them and that there mother was dead. Life was not easy in the United States in the 1930s. Her father often did not have enough money to support them, and the only thing he could do was run an illegal lottery game out of their living quarters. The family lived in fear of the immigration officers and police. All the poverty, hard work, and hardships were worth the dream of education and a better life. After seven years, immigrants were made citizens, and Li Keng's "dream had come true. I was an American now. I loved living in Gold Mountain. Our long journey had been a miracle for me and for my family."

Yang, Belle. *Hannah Is My Name.* Candlewick Press, 2004. ISBN 0-7636-2223-0 Gr. 0–4 Taiwanese

> "Hannah is my name in this new country." Hannah comes to America with her parents from Taiwan. They want her to have a better life and to be free to do anything she chooses. Her family applies for green cards so that they can stay in the United States. In the meantime, her father be very careful that he does not get caught working because he is not supposed to have a job in the United States without a green card; he also earns less than he would with if he were working legally. If he does get caught, their whole family could be sent back to Taiwan. A year goes by and still no green card, until one day Hannah comes home from school and her Mother is making pot

stickers which She only makes on special occasions. For once, Hannah does not sound like a stranger's name now that America is their home.

# Bibliography

Balfassi, Haemi. *Tae's Sonata.* Clarion, 1997. ISBN 0395-84314-6 Gr. 4–6 Korean

Banerjee, Anjali. *Maya Running.* Random House, 2006. ISBN 0-553-49424-4 Gr. 6–8 Asian Indian

Banks, Jacqueline Turner. *A Day for Vincent Chin and Me.* Houghton Mifflin, 2005. ISBN 0-618-54879-3 Gr. 5–9 Japanese

Carlson, Lori M. *American Eyes: New Asian-American Short Stories for Young Adults.* Sagebrush Education Resources, 1996. ISBN 0-7857-9444-1 Gr. 7–12

Cheng, Andrea. *Honeysuckle House.* Boyds Mills, 2004. ISBN 1-886910-99-5 Gr. 3–5 Chinese

_____. *Shanghai Messenger.* Lee & Low, 2005. ISBN 1-58430-238-0 Gr. 3–6 Chinese

Denenberg, Barry. *The Journal of Ben Uchida: Citizen #13559, Mirror Lake Internment Camp.* Scholastic, 2003. ISBN 0-439-55530-2 Juvenile. Japanese

Desai Hidier, Januja. *Born Confused.* Scholastic, 2003. ISBN 0-439-51011-2 Gr. 4–12 Asian Indian

_____. *Fasting, Feasting.* Knopf, 2000. ISBN 0-09-928963–6 Adult. Asian Indian

Fleming, Candace. *Lowji Discovers America.* Simon & Schuster, 2005. ISBN 0-689-86299-7 Gr. 3–5 Asian Indian

Garland, Sherry. *Shadow of the Dragon.* Harcourt Children's Books, 1994. ISBN 0-15-200295-2 Gr. 6–12 Vietnamese

Glenn, Me. *Split Image: A Story in Poems.* HarperCollins, 2002. ISBN 0-06-000481-9 Gr. 8 & up Chinese

Hamanaka, Sheila. *The Journey: Japanese Americans, Racism and Renewal.* Scholastic, 1995. ISBN 0-531-070603 Gr. 4–7 Japanese

Himelblau, Linda. *The Trouble Begins.* Random House Children's Books, 2005 ISBN 0-385-90288-3 Gr. 4–8 Vietnamese

Ho, Minfong. *First Person Fiction: The Stone Goddess.* Scholastic, 2005. ISBN 0-439-38198-3 Juvenile Cambodian

Hoyt-Goldsmith, Diane. *Hoang Anh: A Vietnamese-American Boy.* Holiday House, 1992. ISBN 0-8234-0948-1 Gr. 3–5 Vietnamese

Kadohata, Cynthia. *Kira-Kira.* Simon & Schuster, 2006. ISBN 0-689-85640-7 Gr. 6–9 Japanese

Lee, Lauren. *Stella: On the Edge of Popularity.* Polychrome, 1994. ISBN 1-879965-08-9 Gr. 4–8 Korean

Lee, Marie G. *F Is for Fabuloso.* HarperCollins, 1999. ISBN 0-380-97648-X Gr. 5–9 Korean

_____. *Necessary Roughness.* HarperCollins, 1998. ISBN 0-06-447169-1 Gr. 7 & up Korean

Levine, Ellen. *I Hate English!* Scholastic, 1995. ISBN 0-590-42304-5 Gr. 3–8 Chinese

Look, Lenore. *Ruby Lu, Empress of Everything.* Simon & Schuster, 2006. ISBN 0-689-86460-5 Gr. 1–3 Chinese

Lord, Bette Bao. *In the Year of the Boar and Jackie Robinson.* HarperCollins, 1986. ISBN 0-06-440175-8 Gr. 3–6 Classic Chinese

Ly, Many. *Home Is East.* Delacorte, 2005. ISBN 0-385-73222-8 Gr. 4–6 Cambodian

Mochizuki, Ken. *Beacon Hill Boys.* Scholastic, 2004. ISBN 0-439-24906-5 Gr. 8 & up Japanese

Na, An. *A Step from Heaven.* Penguin Group, 2003. ISBN 0-14-250027-5 Gr. 9–12 Korean

Nagda, Ann Whitehead. *Meow Means Mischief.* Holiday House, 2003. ISBN 0-8234-1786-7 Gr. 4–6 Asian Indian

Namioka, Lensey. *April and the Dragon Lady.* Browndeer Press, 1994. ISBN 0-15-276644-8 Gr. 7 & up Chinese

_____. *Half and Half.* Random House, 2004. ISBN 0-440-41890-9 Gr. 3–7 Chinese Scottish

_____. *Mismatch.* Dell, 2006. ISBN 0-385-73183-3 Gr. 5–9 Chinese Japanese

Okimoto, Jean Davies. *Talent Night.* Sagebrush Education Resources, 2000. ISBN 0-613-83512-3 Gr. 6–10 Japanese

Park, Linda Sue. *Project Mulberry.* Houghton Mifflin, 2005. ISBN 0-618-47786-1 Gr. 5–9 Korean

Patneaude, David. *Thin Wood Walls.* Houghton Mifflin, 2004. ISBN 0-618-34290-7 Gr. 5–9 Japanese

Perkins, Mitali. *The Sunita Experiment.* Hyperion Books, 1994. ISBN 1-56282-671-9 Gr. 5–9 Asian Indian

Salisbury, Graham. *Eyes of the Emperor.* Dell, 2005. ISBN 0-385-90874-1 Gr. 7 & up Japanese

_____. *Under the Blood-Red Sun.* Random House, 2005. ISBN 0-553-49487-2 Gr. 7–10 Japanese

Shea, Pegi Deitz. *Tangled Threads: A Hmong Girl's Story.* Houghton Mifflin, 2003. ISBN 0-618-24748-3 Gr. 6–9 Thai

Smith, Greg Leitich. *Ninjas, Piranhas, and Galileo.* Little, Brown and Company, 2005. ISBN 0-316-01181-9 Gr. 5–8 Japanese

Son, John. *First Person Fiction: Finding My Hat.* Scholastic, 2005. ISBN 0-439-43539-0 Juvenile Korean

Uchida, Yoshiko. *Journey to Topaz.* Heyday Books, 2005. 1-890771-91-0 General Adult Classic Japanese

Wong, Joyce Lee. *Seeing Emily.* Harry N. Abrams, 2005. ISBN 0-8109-5757-4 Gr. 7–11 Chinese

Yang, Gene Luen. *American Born Chinese.* First Second, 2006. ISBN 1-59643-152-0 Juvenile Chinese Graphic Novel

Yee, Lisa. *American Dragons: Twenty-Five Asian American Voices.* HarperCollins, 1995. ISBN 0-06-440603-1 Gr. 7 & up

_____. *Millicent Min, Girl Genius.* Scholastic, 2005. ISBN 0-439-77131-5 Gr. 4–7 Chinese

_____. *Stanford Wong Flunks Big Time.* Scholastic, 2005. ISBN 0-439-62247-6 Gr. 5–7 Chinese

_____. *Tales from Gold Mountain: Stories of the Chinese in the New World.* Groundwood Books, 1999. ISBN 0-88899-098-3 Gr. 7 & up Chinese

Yep, Laurence. *Child of the Owl: Golden Mountain Chronicles, 1965.* HarperCollins, 1990. ISBN 0-06-4403360X Gr. 7 & up Classic Chinese

_____. *The Cook's Family.* Holt, Rinehart & Winston, 1998. ISBN 0-03-992907-8 Gr. 4–7 Chinese

_____. *Thief of Hearts: Golden Mountain Chronicles: 1995.* HarperCollins, 1997. ISBN 0064405915 Gr. 4–6 Chinese

Yoo, David. *Girls for Breakfast.* Random House, 2006. ISBN 0-440-23883-8 Gr. 9 & up Korean

## Picture Books

Bunting, Eve. *So Far from the Sea.* Houghton Mifflin, 1998. ISBN 0-395-72095-8 Gr. 2–5 Japanese

Cheng, Andrea. *Grandfather Counts.* Lee & Low, 2000. ISBN 1-58430-010-8 Gr. K–4 Chinese

_____. *Goldfish and Chrysanthemums.* Lee & Low, 2003. ISBN 1-58430-057-1 Gr. PS–2 Chinese

Chin, Karen. *Sam and the Lucky Money.* Lee & Low Books, 1997. ISBN 1-880000-53-9 Gr. 0–4 Chinese

Chin-Lee, Cynthia. *Almond Cookies and Dragon Well Tea.* Polychrome, 1993. ISBN 1-879965-03-8 Gr. 1–4 Chinese

Choi, Yangsook. *The Name Jar.* Random House Children's Books, 2003. ISBN 0-440-41799-6 Gr. 0–3 Korean

D'Antonio, Nancy. *Our Baby from China: An Adoption Story.* Albert Whitman, 1997. ISBN 0-8075-6162-2 Gr. K–3 Chinese

English, Karen. *Nadia's Hands.* Boyds Mills, 2003. ISBN 1-56397-667-6 Gr. 0–2 Pakistani

Garland, Sherry. *The Lotus Seed.* Harcourt Children's Books, 1997. ISBN 0-15-201483-7 Juvenile Vietnamese

Gilmore, Rachna. *A Gift for Gita.* Tilbury House, 2005. ISBN 0-88448-239-1 Gr. 3–6 Asian Indian

_____. *Lights for Gita.* Tilbury House, 2005. ISBN 0-88448-151-4 Gr. 3–6 Asian Indian

_____. *Roses for Gita.* Tilbury House, 2005. ISBN 0-88448-224-3 Gr. 3–6 Asian Indian

Krishnaswami, Uma. *The Happiest Tree: A Yoga Story.* Lee & Low, 2005. ISBN 1-58430-237-2 Gr.1–4 Asian Indian

Kuklin, Susan. *How My Family Lives in America.* Simon & Schuster, 1998. ISBN 0-689-8221-9 Gr. K–3 African American, Hispanic, Taiwanese

Lin, Grace. *The Ugly Vegetables.* Charlesbridge, 2001. ISBN 1-57091-491-5 Gr. K-3 Chinese

Look, Lenore. *Uncle Peter's Amazing Chinese Wedding*. Simon & Schuster, 2006. ISBN 0-689-84458-1 Juvenile Chinese

McCoy, Karen Kawaamoto. *Bon Odori Dancer*. Polychrome, 1998. ISBN 1-879965-16-X Gr. 1–4 Japanese

Mochizuki, Ken. *Heroes*. Lee & Low, 1997. ISBN 1-880000-50-4 Gr. 2–4 (for older students) Japanese

_____. *How Baseball Saved Us*. Harcourt Trade Publishers, 1995. ISBN 1-880000-19-9 Gr. K–3 Japanese

Pak, Soyung. *Dear Juno*. Penguin Group, 2001. ISBN 0-14-230017-9 Gr. PS–2 Korean

_____. *Sumi's First Day of School Ever*. Penguin Group, 2003. ISBN 0-670-03522-X Gr. K–3 Korean

Park, Frances, and Ginger Park. *The Have a Good Day Café*. Lee & Low, 2005. ISBN 1-58430-171-6 Gr. 1–3 Korean

Park, Linda Sue, and Julia Durango. *Yum! Yuck! A Foldout Book of People Sounds*. Charlesbridge, 2005. 1-57091-659-4 Gr. PS-7

Peacock, Carol Antoinette. *Mommy Far, Mommy Near: An Adoption Story*. Albert Whitman, 2000. ISBN 0-8075-5234-8 Gr. K–4 Chinese

Rattigan, Jama Kim. *Dumpling Soup*. Little, Brown and Company, 1998. ISBN 0-316-73047-1 Gr. PS–3 Korean-Chinese-Japanese-Hawaiian-Anglo

Recorvits, Helen. *My Name Is Yoon*. Farrar, Straus & Giroux, 2003. ISBN 0-374-35114-7 Gr. 0–3 Korean

Say, Allen. *Allison*. Houghton Mifflin, 2004. ISBN 0-618-49537-1 Gr. 0–3 Japanese

_____. *Grandfather's Journey*. Houghton Mifflin, 1993. ISBN 0-395-57035-7 Gr. 0–3 Japanese

Thong, Roseanne. *Round Is a Mooncake*. Chronicle Books, 2000. 0-8118-2676-7 Gr. PS–0 Chinese

Trottier, Maxine. *The Walking Stick*. Stoddart Kids, 1999. ISBN 0-7737-3101-6 Gr. 0–3 Vietnamese

Uchida, Yoshiko. *The Bracelet*. Penguin Group, 1996. ISBN 0-689-11390-X Gr. PS–3 Japanese

Uegaki, Chieri. *Suki's Kimono*. Kids Can Press, 2003. ISBN 1-55337-752-4 Gr. 1–3 Japanese

Wong, Janet S. *Apple Pie Fourth of July*. Harcourt Children's Books, 2006. ISBN 0-15-205708-0 Gr. PS–2 Chinese

_____. *This Next New Year*. Farrar, Straus & Giroux, 2000. ISBN 0-374-35503-7 Gr. PS–2 Chinese

Yashima, Taro. *Crow Boy*. Penguin Group, 1976. ISBN 0-14-050172-X Gr. PK–3 Classic Japanese

Yin. *Coolies*. Penguin Group, 2003. ISBN 0-14-250055-0 Gr. 3–6

## Nonfiction

Aihara, Chris. *Nikkei Donburi: A Japanese American Cultural Survival Guide*. Polychrome, 2004. ISBN 1-879965-18-6 Gr. 1-4

Bryan, Nichol. *Filipino Americans.* ABDO, 2004. ISBN 1-57765-988-0 Gr. 0-6

Cha, Dia. *Dia's Story Cloth: The Hmong People's Journey of Freedom.* Minnesota Humanities Commission, 2002. ISBN 1-931016-11-9 Juvenile

Heinrichs, Ann. *Chinese New Year.* Child's World, 2006. ISBN 1-59296-572-5 Juvenile

Hoobler, Dorothy. *The Japanese American Family Album.* Oxford University Press, 1998. ISBN 0-19-512423–5 Young Adult

Hoyt-Goldsmith, Diane. *Celebrating Chinese New Year.* Holiday House, 1998. ISBN 0-8234-1393-4 Gr. 4–6

Ishizuka, Kathy. *Asian-American Authors.* Enslow, 2000. ISBN 0-7660-1376-6 Gr. 6–12

Kerns, Ann. *Japanese in America.* Lerner, 2006. ISBN 0-8225-3952-7 Gr. 4–7

Krasno, Rena. *Kneeling Carabao and Dancing Giants: Celebrating Filipino Festivals.* Pacific View Press, 1997. ISBN 1-881896-15-3 Gr. 4–8

MacMillan, Diane M. *Tet: Vietnamese New Year.* Enslow, 1994. ISBN 0-89490-501-5 Gr. 1–4

Mayeda, Gene H. *Children of Asian America.* Polychrome, 1996. ISBN 1-879965-15-7 Gr. 5 & up

Nam, Vickie. *A Yell-Oh Girls! Emerging Voices Explore Culture, Identity and Growing Up Asian.* Sagebrush Education Resources, 2001. ISBN 0-613-49389-3 Gr. 7–12

Oppenheim, Joanne. *Dear Miss Breed.* Scholastic, 2006. ISBN 0-439-56992-3 Gr. 6 & up

Shalant, Phyllis. *Look What We've Brought You from India: Crafts, Games, Recipes, Stories and Other Cultural Activities from Indian Americans.* Silver Burdett Press, 1997. ISBN 0-382-39463-1 Juvenile

_____. *Look What We've Brought You from Korea: Crafts, Games, Recipes, Stories and Other Cultural Activities from Korean Americans.* Silver Burdett Press, 1994. ISBN 0-671-88701-7 Juvenile

_____. *Look What We've Brought You from Vietnam: Crafts, Games, Recipes, Stories and Other Cultural Activities from Vietnamese Americans.* Silver Burdett Press, 1998. ISBN 0-382-39982-X Juvenile

Sinnot, Susan. *Extraordinary Asian-Pacific Americans.* Scholastic Library, 2003. ISBN 0-516-29355-9 Gr. 6 & up

Stepanchuk, Carol. *Exploring Chinatown: A Children's Guide to Chinese Culture.* Pacific View Press, 2003. ISBN 1-881896-25-0 Gr. 4-8

Taus-Bolstad, Stacey. *Koreans in America.* Lerner, 2005. ISBN 0-8225-4874-7 Gr. PS–7

Tran, Barbara. *Watermark: Vietnamese American Poetry and Prose.* Asian American Writers' Workshop, 1998. ISBN 1-889876-05-4 No level

## Series

*The Asian American Experience Series.* Chelsea House

*Asian Arts and Crafts for Creative Kids Series.* Tuttle

# Discussion Questions

- How does the main character deal with being torn between two countries?

- Could the Internment ever happen again?

- How are prisons and interment camps alike and different?

- Do you believe that all Asians are very intelligent?

- How have Asians influence U.S. culture?

- Are there any Asian words that have become part of our culture?

- What are you favorite Asian foods?

# Featured Author

## Linda Sue Park

**Birthplace:** Urbana, Illinois
**Date of Birth:** March 25, 1960
**Current Home:** Upstate New York
**Titles**

*Archer's Quest.* (2006)

*Bee-bim Bop!* (2005)

*Project Mulberry* (2005)

*What Does Bunny See? A Book of Colors and Flowers* (2005)

*Yum! Yuck! A Foldout Book of People Sounds.* (2005)

*The Firekeeper's Son* (2004)

*Mung-Mung: A Foldout Book of Animal Sounds* (2004)

*When My Name Was Keoko* (2002)

*A Single Shard* (2001)

*The Kite Fighters* (2000)

*Seesaw Girl.* (1999)

### Interesting Information

- The daughter of Korean immigrants, Linda Sue has been writing poems and stories since she was four years old, and her favorite thing to do as a child was read.

- She had her first piece of poetry, a haiku, published in a children's magazine when she was nine years old.

- She was paid $1 for the story, and she gave it to her father for Christmas. Her father never cashed the check of one dollar. Instead he had it framed and still has it today.

- Log on to Linda Sue's Web site, and you have access to her live journal of day-to-day happenings, including pictures, books she is reading, and her thoughts about what she is doing at that moment.

**Web Site:** www.lspark.com

**Contact:** If you would like the author's autograph, a signed bookplate, or a reply to your letter, write to the address below with your request and enclose a self-addressed stamped envelope!

Linda Sue Park
c/o Clarion Books
215 Park Avenue South
New York NY 10003

*Please note:* The author will not respond to e-mails or messages in "my guestbook," but she will reply to letters sent through the mail.

# Annotated Journal Article

Kim, Won. "Asian Americans Are at the Head of the Class." *Diversity* (July/August 2006): 40–43.

Statistics prove that Asian Americans score higher on the SATs in math than any other demographic group, make up 16 percent of the students at Ivy League schools, and have the highest percentage of people with a bachelor's degree.

However, all Asian Americans are not the same. A higher percentage of Asian Americans have not graduated from high school than whites. Immigrants from countries that are agriculturally versus technologically based are less likely to excel because education is not emphasized by their cultures. Those who are excelling are first-generation Asian Americans who see the sacrifices their parents have made and grew up with the idea of going to the best school. Religion, such as Hindu, which values education also is an influence. In the future, Asian Americans may not excel in the classroom because of their assimilation into American culture.

# Resources

## Books

Engelbert, Phillis. *American Civil Rights: Almanac.* UXL, 1999. ISBN 0-7876-3178-2

Sinnott, Susan. *Extraordinary Asian Americans and Pacific Islanders.* Children's Press, 2003. ISBN 0-516-22655-X

Williams, Richard, and Kedar Nath Dwivedi. *Meeting the Needs of Ethnic Minority Children.* Jessica Kingsley, 2002. ISBN 1-85302-959-9

## Organizations

Asian American Legal Defense and Education Fund
99 Hudson St., 12th Floor
New York, NY 10013-2869
Phone 212-966-5932
www.apa2000.org

## Web Sites

**South Asia and the South Asian Diaspora in Children's Literature: An annotated bibliography, a work in progress:** http://www.poojamakhijani.com/sakidlit.html

**Cynthia Leitich Smith Web site that includes bibliographies on Chinese Americans, Korean Americans, and Japanese Americans:** http://www.cynthialeitichsmith.com/index.html

**Official Publisher's Web site for Author Allen Say:** http://www.houghtonmifflinbooks.com/authors/allensay

**Laurence Yep Official Web page:** http://www.harpercollins.com/authorintro/index.asp?authorid+12929

**Welcome to the World of Rachna Gilmore:** www.rachnagilmore.ca

**Author and former Miss America:** http://www.lisayee.com

**Welcome to the Fire Escape! A safe place to think, chat, and read about life between cultures:** Mitali Perkins: http://www.mitaliperkins.com

# Awards

## Asian Pacific American Award for Literature (APAAL)

Founded in 1980 and formally affiliated with the American Library Association in 1982, this organization was established to meet the needs of Asian Pacific Librarians and those who serve the Asian Pacific community.

The Asian Pacific American Librarians Association and Chinese American Librarians Association started this award in 1998. The APAAL award honors adult fiction and nonfiction, children's and young adult authors and illustrators of books that deal with Asians and Asian Americans. See http://www.apalaweb.org/awards/awards.htm.

### *Illustration in Children Literature Winner 2004–2005*

Park, Linda Sue, and Julie Downing (Illustrator). *The Firekeeper's Son.* 2004.

### *Honorable Mention for Illustration in Children Literature: 2004–2005*

Yoo, Paula, and Dom Lee (Illustrator). *Sixteen Years in Sixteen Seconds: The Sammy Lee Story.* 2005.

Lipp, Frederick, and Jason Gaillard (Illustrator). *Bread Song.* 2004.

### *Text in Children and Young Adult Literature Winner: 2004–2005*

Kadohata, Cynthia. *Kira Kira*. 2004.

### *Honorable Mention for Text in Children and Young Adult Literature: 2004–2005*

Cheng, Andrea. *Shanghai Messenger*. 2005.

Park, Linda Sue. *Project Mulberry: A Novel*. 2005.

# Chapter 6

# Biracial/Multiracial

## Introduction

A sharp rise in interracial marriages has prompted a "positive awareness of interracial and multicultural identity" (Association of MultiEthnic Americans). A multiracial category was included on the 2000 census, and 7 million selected this as the racial/ethnic background. However, multiracial youth are not recognized on forms or in diversity curriculum. Some criticize certain organizations that lobby for more awareness for biracial are escaping from being "black." In the meantime, multiracial children have the highest rates of physical and sexual abuse of any racial group and are among the fastest-growing segments entering the juvenile justice system.

## Definition

**Multiracial:** "Two or more races" refers to combinations of two or more of the following race categories: White, Black or African American, American Indian and Alaska Native, Asian, Native Hawaiian and Other Pacific Islander, some other race. (Magazine Publishers of America)

# Annotations

Agard, John. *Half-caste and Other Poems.* Hodder Children's Books, 2004. ISBN 0-340-89382-6 Gr. 9 & up

>This English poet includes many poems of diversity: "And All Was Good," "My Move Your Move," and "Half-caste, a Marriage of Opposites" are just a few.

Crutcher, Chris. *Whale Talk.* HarperCollins, 2001. ISBN 0-688-18019-1 Gr. 8 & up

>T. J. was adopted when he was two years old. His racial makeup is white, black, and Japanese. His hometown is in the northeast region of Washington and western Idaho, and he is not always accepted. T. J. cannot stand idly by when an injustice occurs. His favorite teacher asks him to put together a swim team for his high school. T. J. selects the misfits of the school; this becomes a thorn in the side of the schools' jocks. They are determined that the swim team members will not receive a letter in their sport. The team bonds, and all benefit, but the price will be high for T. J. Soon he will realize how risky it is to act like an adult.

Frank, E. R. *America.* Simon Pulse, 2003. ISBN 0-689-85772-0 Gr. 8 & up

>America is just like the country: he isn't black, he isn't white, he is a little bit of everything. America was living with a foster mother, Mrs. Harper, and when he is taken to visit his natural mother, the system forgot about him, and he was lost for many years. When he was eight, he was sent back to Mrs. Harper, but now America thinks of himself as bad. Mr. Browning, who takes care of Mrs. Harper, befriends the vulnerable America. When he takes advantage of America, America does the unthinkable and regresses into his safe place, not caring if he lives or dies.

# Bibliography

Bell, William. *Zack.* Simon & Schuster, 1999. ISBN 0-689-82248-0 Gr. 6 & up

Forrester, Sandra. *Dust from Old Bones.* William Morrow, 1999. ISBN 0-688-16202-9 Gr. 6–9

Hamilton, Virginia. *Plain City.* Scholastic, 1993. ISBN 0-590-47364-6 Gr. 7 & up

Headley, Justina Chen. *Nothing but the Truth (And a Few White Lies).* Little, Brown and Company, 2006. ISBN 0-316-01128-2 Gr. 5–9

Little, Kimberley Griffiths. *The Last Snake Runner.* Knopf, 2002. ISBN 0-375-81539-2 Gr. 6–9

McFerrin, Linda Watanabe. *Namako: Sea Cucumber.* Coffee House Press, 1998. ISBN 1-56689-05-6 Young Adult

McKay, Lawrence, Jr. *Journey Home.* Lee & Low, 2000. ISBN 1-58430-005-1 Gr. PS–5

McNamee, Graham. *Nothing Wrong with a Three-Legged Dog.* Random House, 2001. ISBN 0-440-41687-6 Gr. 3–7

Murphy, Rita. *Black Angels.* Delacorte, 2001. ISBN 0-385-32776-5 Gr. 5–7

Nye, Naomi Shihab. *Habibi.* Simon & Schuster, 1997. 0-689-80149-1 Gr. 7 & up

O'Connor, Barbara. *Me and Rupert Goody*. Farrar, Straus & Giroux, 1999. ISBN 0-374-34904-5 Gr. 4–7

Osa, Nancy. *Cuba 15*. Random House, 2003. ISBN 0-385-73021-7 Young Adult

Osborne, Mary Pope. *Adaline Falling Star*. Scholastic, 2000. ISBN 0-439-05947-X Gr. 5–8

Patrick, Denise Lewis. *The Longest Ride*. Holt, 1999. ISBN 0-8050-4715-8 Gr. 6-9

Rodowsky, Colby F. *That Fernhill Summer*. Farrar, Straus & Giroux, 2006. ISBN 0-374-37442-2 Gr. 5–8

Rosten, Carrie. *Cloe Leiberman (Sometimes Wong)*. Random House, 2005. ISBN 0-385-73247-3 Gr. 7 & up

Shim, Sun Yung. *Cooper's Lesson*. Children's Book Press, 2004. ISBN 0-89239-193-6 Gr. 3–5

Taylor, Mildred. *The Land*. Phyllis Fogelman, 2001. ISBN 0-8037-1950-7 Gr. 7 & up

Viglucci, Patricia Costa. *Sun Dance at Turtle Rock*. Stone Pine, 1996. ISBN 0-9645914-9 Gr. 5–8

Werlin, Nancy. *Black Mirror*. Dial, 2001. ISBN 0-14-250028-3 Young Adult

Wilson, Diane Lee. *Black Storm Comin'*. Simon & Schuster, 2006. ISBN 0-689-87138-4 Gr. 7–10

Woodson, Jacqueline. *Behind You*. Puffin, 2006. ISBN 0-14-240390-3 Young Adult

Wyeth, Sharon Dennis. *The World of Daughter McGuire*. Random House, 2001. ISBN 0-375-89502-7 Gr. 4–6

Yep, Laurence. *Child of the Owl*. HarperCollins, 1990. ISBN 0-06-440336-X Gr. 7 & up

## Picture Books

Ada, Alma Flor. *I Love Saturdays y Domingos*. Simon & Schuster, 2004. ISBN 0-689-87409-X Gr. K–2

Adoff, Arnold. *Black Is Brown Is Tan*. HarperCollins, 1973, reissued 2002. ISBN 0-06-028776-4 Gr. PS–3 Classic

Ahlberg, Janet and Allan. *Starting School*. Puffin, 1988. ISBN 0-14-050843-0 Gr. PS–2

Cheng, Andrea. *Grandfather Counts*. Lee & Low, 2003. ISBN 1-58430-158-9 Gr. K–3

Cole, Heidi, and Nancy Vogl. *Am I a Color Too?* Illumination Arts, 2005. ISBN 0-9740190-5-4 Gr. PS–3

Davol, Marguerite W. *Black, White, Just Right!* Albert Whitman, 1993. ISBN 0-8075-0785-7 Gr. PS–2

Edmonds, Lyra. *An African Princess*. Corgi Books, 2005. ISBN 0-552-55033-7 Gr. PS–2

Friedman, Ian. *How My Parents Learned to Eat*. Houghton Mifflin, 1984. ISBN 0-395-35379-3 Gr. K–3

Gonzales-Sullaway, Natalie. *Sungka and Smiling Irish Eyes, a Boy Discovers What It Means to Be Half-Irish and Half-Filipino*. BookSurge, 2003. ISBN 1-59457-101-5 Juvenile

Igus, Toyomi. *Two Mrs. Gibsons*. Children's Book Press, 1996. ISBN 0-89239-135-9 Gr. K–3

Iijima, Geneva Cobb. *The Way We Do It in Japan.* Albert Whitman, 2002. ISBN 0-8075-7822-3 Gr. K–3

Jenness, Aylette. *Families: A Celebration of Diversity, Commitment and Love.* Turtleback Books, 1989. ISBN 0-606-05829-X Juvenile

Johnston, Tony. *Angel City.* Philomel, 2006. ISBN 0-399-23405-7 Juvenile

Katz, Karen. *The Colors of Us.* Henry Holt, 2002. ISBN 0-8050-7163-6 Gr. PS–3

Kissinger, Katie. *All the Colors We Are: The Story of How We Get Our Skin Color.* Redleaf Press, 1994. ISBN 0-934140-80-4 Gr. PS–5

Mandelbaum, Pili. *You Be Me I'll Be You.* Sagebrush Education Resources, 1993. ISBN 0-613-87692-6 Gr. K–3

McGill, Alice. *Molly Bannaky.* Houghton Mifflin, 1999. ISBN 0-395-72287-X Gr. 0–3

Monk, Isabel. *Hope.* Lerner Publishing Group, 2004. ISBN 1-57505-792-1 Gr. PS–3

Polacco, Patricia. *Chicken Sunday.* Penguin Group, 1998. ISBN 0-698-11615-1 Gr. 1–3

Say, Allen. *Allison.* Houghton Mifflin, 2004. ISBN 0-618-49537-1 Gr. 0–3

Williams, Vera B. *More, More, More, Said the Baby: Three Love Stories.* HarperCollins, 1997. ISBN 0-688-15634-7 Gr. 1–7

Wing, Natasha. *Jalapeno Bagels.* Simon & Schuster, 1995. ISBN 0-02-793077-7 Gr. K–3

Wong, Janet S. *This Next New Year.* Farrar, Straus & Giroux, 2000. ISBN 0-374-35503-6 Gr. PS–3

## Nonfiction

Brill, Marlene Targ. *Barack Obama: Working to Make a Difference.* Lerner, 2006. ISBN 0-8225-3417-7 Gr. 5–8

Cruz, Barbara. *Multiethnic Teens and Cultural Identity.* Enslow, 2001. ISBN 0-7660-1201-8 Gr. 6 & up

Gaskins, Pearl Fuyo, ed. *What Are You: Voices of Mixed-Race Young People.* Henry Holt, 1999. ISBN 0-8050-5968-7 Gr. 8 & up

Lanier, Shannon, and Jane Feldman. *Jefferson's Children: The Story of One American Family.* Random House, 2000. ISBN 0-375-80597-4 Gr. 6 & up

McCutcheon, John. *Happy Adoption Day.* Little, Brown and Company, 2001. ISBN 0-316-60323-6 Gr. PS–1

Nash, Gary B. *Forbidden Love: The Secret History of Mixed-Race America.* Henry Holt, 1999. ISBN 0-8050-4953-3 Gr. 9–12

O'Hearn, Claudine C. *Half and Half: Writers on Growing Up Biracial and Bicultural.* Henry Holt, 1999. ISBN 0-8050-4953-3 Gr. 9–12

Senisi, Ellen B. *For My Family, Love, Allie.* Albert Whitman, 1998. ISBN 0-8075-2539-1 Gr. PS–2

Tallchief, Maria, and Rosemary Wells. *Tallchief: America's Prima Ballerina.* Viking, 1999. ISBN 0-670-88756-0 Gr. 2–6

# Discussion Questions

- Do you think it is a good idea to have a biracial category on the Census? Why or why not?

- Should a biracial category be included on all forms? Why or why not?

- Why do you think biracial children are the fastest-growing segment entering the juvenile justice system?

- What issues do you think biracial children have to deal with?

# Featured Author

## Andrea Cheng

**Birthplace:** Cincinnati, Ohio
**Date of Birth:** September 19, 1957
**Current Home:** Cincinnati, Ohio
**Titles**

*Eclipse* (2006)

*Lemon Sisters* (2006)

*Lacy Dowry* (2005)

*Shanghai Messenger* (2005)

*When the Bees Fly Home* (2005)

*Grandfather Counts* (2004)

*Honeysuckle House* (2004)

*Anna and the Bookbinder* (2003)

*Goldfish and Chrysanthemums* (2003)

*The Key Collection* (2003)

*Marika* (1998)

**Interesting Information**

- Andrea Cheng's parents are from Hungary, and they immigrated to the United States in 1954.

- She grew up in Cincinnati, Ohio, and moved back there after she was married to live closer to her parents.

- She met her future husband, Jim, at Cornell University in Ithaca, New York.

- Jim is the son of Chinese Immigrants, and both sets of parents share many of the same values. They have three children.

**Web Site:** http://www.andreacheng.com/

**Contact:** (E-mail) cheng@frontstreetbooks.com

# Annotated Journal Article

Okota, Junko and Shari Frost. "Multiracial Characters in Children's Literature." *Book Links.* (December 2002/January 2003): 51–57.

The lines of color are blurring, but the characters in literature do not reflect this trend. Biracial children have a difficult time identifying with the illustrations in books. Sometimes the illustrations may include multiracial children, but the text does not. Others allude to a multiracial background but do not directly address it. The issues of biracial heritage is more likely discussed in books for older children. The article includes a list for educators and students "so that we may all increase our awareness of the issues both embraced and faced by people of mixed racial heritage."

# Resources

## Books

Rockquemore, Kerry. *Raising Biracial Children.* AltaMira Press, 2005. ISBN 0-7591-0900-1 General Adult

Wright, Marguerite. *I'm Chocolate, You're Vanilla: Raising Healthy Black and Biracial Children in a Race-Conscious World.* John Wiley & Sons, 2000. ISBN 0-7879-5234-6 General Adult

## Organizations

Association of MultiEthnic Americans (AMEA)
PO Box 66061
Tucson, AZ 85728-6061
http://www.ameasite.org

Project RACE
2910 Kerry Forest Parkway, D4
Tallahassee, FL 32308
FAX: (850) 894-8540
http://www.projectrace.com

## Web Sites

**Interracial and Multiracial links:** http://multirace.org/multirace.htm

**Association of MultiEthnic Americans:** http://www.ameasite.org/

**Tolerance.org:** http://tolerance.org/teach (This site is sponsored by the Southern Poverty Law Center and promotes tolerance and teaching against hatred.)

# Chapter 7

# Latino (Latin America)/ Hispanic (Spanish)

## Introduction

Hispanic immigration has followed the same patterns as the earlier immigration of the Irish, Italian, and Jewish immigrants. The major difference is that most Hispanics do not have to cross an ocean to get here. Many Americans are concerned that the United States cannot assimilate this large of a group. Mexican immigration is blurring the 2,000-mile border between the United States and Mexico. Every immigrating group has had an effect on the culture, and its impact is greatest in the areas of the largest concentrations. In 2002, there were 37.4 million Hispanics in the United Sates, comprising 13 percent of the total population; of this total, 25 million were Mexican American. This mass migration from Mexico began in 1970 and doubled in ten years. It is projected that by 2050, the Hispanic population will rise to 24.4 percent of the population. The major motivation for immigration is employment. Now it appears that births, not immigration, will account for the major increase in population. Although the number of Hispanics is greater than any other immigrating group of people, they are usually poor and have few opportunities for upward mobility.

# Definition

**Hispanic:** People who identify with the terms "Hispanic" or "Latino" are those who classify themselves in on of the specific Hispanic or Latino categories—"Mexican," "Puerto Rican," or "Cuban"—as well as those who indicate that they are "other Spanish, Hispanic, or Latino." Origin can be viewed as the heritage, nationality group, lineage, or country of birth of the person or the person's parents or ancestors before their arrival in the United States. People who identify their origin as Spanish, Hispanic, or Latino may be of any race. (Magazine Publishers of America)

# Annotations

Abraham, Susan Gonzales, and Denise Gonzales. *Surprising Cecilia.* Cinco Puntos, 2006. ISBN 0-938317-96-2 Gr. 6–10 Mexican

Cecilia knows that her family wants what is best for her, but sometimes she feels her mother doesn't understand her. There is always so much work to be done around the house, taking care of her younger brothers and sisters, before she can begin to think about her schoolwork. Cecilia is allowed to go to high school as long as her brother goes as well. Her mother is slow to change and wants to keep Cecilia safe and away from the influence of the "town girls." Cecilia realizes how hard her mother works, and even though they are poor, she is rich because her family is willing to share their goods and love. Each chapter is its own short story of the life of a young Mexican American girl.

Canales, Viola. *The Tequila Worm.* Random House, 2005. ISBN 0-385-74674-1 Gr. 5–8 Mexican

Clara, the storyteller, visits all of the homes in the barrio, and one day she tells Sofia that she is like her great-great-grandmother—a mule always kicking her way through life. This will be true for Sofia as well. When she is in grade school and one girl is particularly mean, calling Sofia names like "Taco Head," the coach said the best way to get back is to kick "her butt at school, by beating her in English, math, everything—even sports." This is what Sophia does, and it leads to her receiving a scholarship to a prestigious boarding school, Saint Luke's, which is 350 miles away. Sofia has to ask permission to attend the school from each member of her family. She is allowed to go, but she must work on being a good *comadre,* "someone who makes people into a family."

Colato Lainez, Rene. *I Am Rene, the Boy/Soy Rene, El Niño.* Arte Publico Press, 2005. ISBN 1-55885-378-2 Gr. PS–2 El Salvadoran

The author based this bilingual book on his own experience. In the book, Rene is from El Salvador, and when the teacher at school calls roll, a girl also responds to the name Rene. The little boy then realizes that his name is also a girl's name, and the other boys tease him. Rene researches his name and enters an essay contest, writing about the origin of his name and what it means to him. He wins the contest.

Elya, Susan Middleton. *Bebe Goes Shopping.* Harcourt, 2006. ISBN0-15-205426-X Gr. PS General Hispanic

A Mama and her little Bebe go for a quick trip to the supermarket, or *supermercado.* The experience is familiar, and the use of Spanish is intertwined. The Bebe increasingly becomes a handful until he receives his snack for the day, a box of *caja,* circus animal cookies.

Jaramillo, Ann. *La Linea.* Roaring Brook Press, 2006. ISBN 1-59643-154-7 Gr. 5 & up Mexican
    When Miguel is fifteen, he receives a long-awaited letter from his Papa. It is time—Papa has finally saved enough money to arrange a safe passage across the border to the United States. Shortly, Miguel will be shocked to learn that his younger sister Elena had disguised herself, and she, too, is determined to travel north. There will be many hardships, sandstorms, encounters with violent gangs, and death before Miguel and Elena stumble toward the road that cuts across the desert, leading to California.

# Bibliography

Alvarez, Julia. *How the Garcia Girls Lost Their Accents.* Penguin, 2005. ISBN 0-452-28707-3 General Adult Dominican

Ancona, George. *Barrio: José's Neighborhood/Barrio: El Barrio de José.* Harcourt, 1998. ISBN 0-15-201049-1 Gr. 3–6 Mexican

Cisneros, Sandra. *The House on Mango Street.* Random House, 1994. ISBN 0-679-43335-X General Adult Mexican

Cofer, Judith Ortiz. *Call Me Maria.* Scholastic, 2004. ISBN 0-439-38577-6 Gr. 4–7 Puerto Rico

_____. *An Island Like You: Stories of the Barrio.* Puffin, 1995. ISBN 0-14-038068-X Gr. 7–12 Puerto Rican

Fogelin, Adrian. *The Big Nothing.* Peachtree, 2004. ISBN 1-56145-388-9 Gr. 7–9

Galarza, Ernesto. *Barrio Boy.* Holt, Rinehart & Winston, 2000. ISBN 0-03-055987-1 Gr. 6–9 Mexican

Herrera, Juan Felipe. *CrashBoomLove: A Novel in Verse.* University of New Mexico Press, 1999. ISBN 0-8263-2114-3 Gr. 9–12 Chicano

Hobbs, Will. *Crossing the Wire.* HarperCollins, 2006. ISBN 0-06-074139-2 Gr. 5 & up Mexican

Jimenez, Francisco. *Breaking Through.* Houghton Mifflin, 2001. ISBN 0-618-01173-0 Gr. 5–8 Mexican

_____. *The Circuit: Stories from the Life of a Migrant Child.* Houghton Mifflin, 1997. ISBN 0-8263-179-9 Gr. 5 & up Mexican

Lupica, Mike. *Heat.* Puffin, 2007. ISBN 0-14-240757-7 Gr. 5–8 Mexican

Martinez, Victor. *Parrot in the Oven Mi Vida.* HarperCollins, 1996. ISBN 0-06-026704-6 Gr. 7–10 Mexican

Osa, Nancy. *Cuba 15.* Random House, 2003. ISBN 0-385-73021-7 Gr. 6–10 Cuban-Polish

Rodriguez, Luis J. *America Is Her Name.* Curbstone, 1998. ISBN 1-880684-40-3 Gr. 2–6 Mexican

Ryan, Pam Muñoz. *Becoming Naomi León.* Scholastic, 2004. ISBN 0-439-26969-5 Gr. 4–7 Mexican

_____. *Esperanza Rising.* Scholastic, 2000. ISBN 0-439-12041-1 Gr. 5–8 Mexican

Saenz, Benjamin Alire. *Sammy and Juliana in Hollywood.* Cinco Puntos Press, 2004. ISBN 0-93831-81-4 Young Adult Mexican

Saldana, Rene. *The Jumping Tree.* Delacorte, 2001. ISBN 0-385-32725-0 Gr. 7–12 Mexican

Santiago, Esmeraldo. *When I Was Puerto Rican.* Da Capo Press, 2006. ISBN 0-306-81452-8 Young Adult Puerto Rican

Seena, Danzy. *Caucasia: A Novel.* Penguin, 1999. ISBN 0-613-14618-2 Gr 7–12 Young Adult (for mature readers)

Thomas, Piri. *Down These Mean Streets.* Knopf, 1997. ISBN 0-679-78142-0 General Adult Puerto Rican

Triana, Gaby. *Cubanita.* HarperCollins, 2006. ISBN 0-06-056022-3 Gr. 10 & up Cuban

Veciana-Suarez, Ana. *Flight to Freedom.* Scholastic, 2002. ISBN 0-439-38199-1 Gr. 6–9 Cuban

## Picture Books

Ancona, George. *Mi Barrio: My Neighborhood.* Scholastic Library, 2005. ISBN 0-516-25064-7 Gr. 1–3 Mexican

Anzaldua, Gloria. *Friends from the Other Side.* Sagebrush Education Resources, 1995. ISBN 0-613-00028-5 Gr. 0–3 Mexican

Garza, Carmen Lomas. *In My Family: Paintings and Stories/En Mi Familia: Cuadros y Relatos.* Children's Book Press, 2000. Gr. K–3 Mexican

Jimenez, Francisco. *La Mariposa.* DIANE, 2004. ISBN 0-7567-8433-6 PS–4 Mexican

Johnston, Tony. *Uncle Rain Cloud.* Charlesbridge, 2001. ISBN 0-88106-371-1 Gr. 1–4 Mexican

Mora, Pat. *The Rainbow Tulip.* Penguin Group, 2003. ISBN 0-14-250009-7 Gr. K–3 Mexican

_____. *Tomas and the Library Lady.* Knopf, 1997. ISBN 0-679-80401-3 Gr. PS–3 Mexican

O'Neill, Alexis. *Estela's Swap.* Lee & Low, 2002. ISBN 1-58430-044-2 Gr. PS–2 Mexican

Perez, Amada Irma. *My Very Own Room/Mi Propio Cuartito.* Children's Book Press, 2000. ISBN 0-89239-164-2 Gr. 1–3 Mexican

Perez, L. King. *First Day in Grapes.* Lee & Low, 2002. ISBN 1-58430-0450-0 Gr. 1–3 Mexican

Russell, Barbara Timberlake. *The Remembering Stone.* Farrar, Straus & Giroux, 2004. ISBN 0-374-36242-4 Gr. PS–2 Costa Rican

Velasquez, Eric. *Grandma's Records.* Walker, 2001. ISBN 0-8027-8760-6 Gr. K–3 Puerto Rican

## Nonfiction

Argueta, Jorge. *A Movie in My Pillow/Una Pelicula en Mi Almohada.* Children's Book Press, 2001. ISBN 0-89239-165-0 Gr. 4–8 El Salvadoran

Brown, Monica. *My Name Is Celia: The Life of Celia Cruz.* Northland, 2004. ISBN 0-87358-872-X Gr. 2–4 Cuban

Krull, Kathleen. *Harvesting Hope: The Story of Cesar Chavez.* Harcourt, 2003. ISBN 0-15-201437-3 Gr. 3 & up Mexican

Shalant, Phyllis. *Look What We've Brought You from Mexico: Crafts, Games, Recipes, Stories and Other Cultural Activities from Mexican Americans.* Silver Burdett Press, 1998. ISBN 0-382-39979-X Juvenile

_____. *Look What We've Brought You from the Caribbean: Crafts, Games, Recipes, Stories and Other Cultural Activities.* Silver Burdett Press, 1998. ISBN 0-382-39926-9 Juvenile

## Series

*Fact Finders Biographies: Great Hispanics.* Capstone Press Books. Gr. 2–3

*Hispanic Biographies.* Enslow. Gr. 2–3

*The Great Hispanic Heritage.* Chelsea House. Gr. 6–12

*Latino Biography Library.* Enslow. Gr. 6 & up

*Latinos in the Limelight.* Chelsea House. ISBN 0-7910-8728-X Gr. 4–8

# Discussion Questions

- Do you think that the United States should have two languages based on the increasing growth of its Hispanic population?
- Should Spanish be taught to all students?
- What effect has the Hispanic/Latino culture had on you?

# Featured Author

## Pam Muñoz Ryan

**Birthplace:** Bakersfield, California
**Date of Birth:** December 25, 1951
**Current Home:** Leucadia, California
**Titles**

*Becoming Naomi León* (2006)

*Nacho and Lolita* (2005)

*There Was No Snow on Christmas Eve* (2005)

*How Do You Raise a Raisin* (2004)

*A Box of Friends* (2003)

*Mud Is Cake* (2002)

*Hello Ocean* (2001)

*Mice and Beans* (2001)

*Esperanza Rising* (2000)

*A Pinky Is a Baby Mouse* (1999)

*Amelia & Eleanor Go for a Ride* (1999)

*Riding Freedom* (1999)

*The Funnie Family Vacation* (1998)

*A Pinky Is a Baby Mouse* (1997)

*California Here We Come!* (1997)

*The Crayon Counting Book* (1996)

*One Hundred Is a Family* (1994)

*The Flag We Love* (1992)

**Interesting Information**

- Pam is Spanish, Mexican, Basque, Italian, and Oklahoman.

- She has written more than twenty-five books for children of all ages, including picture books to titles for young adults.

- She lives six blocks from the ocean with her four children and two dogs.

**Web Site:** http://www.pammunozyran.com

**Contact:**
Pam Muñoz Ryan
C/O Scholastic
557 Broadway
New York, NY 10012-3999
E-mail: PMunozRyan@aol.com

# Annotated Journal Articles

Negroni, Peter. "The New Wave: Immigration in the Classroom." *The College Board Review* (spring 2006): 42–43.

This article focuses on the influx of Hispanic/Latino people to the United States and how this is causing a demographic shift of huge proportions. To make a better life for themselves, it is imperative that these young people enter and remain in college. The College Board has created a Latino Initiative for school reform to improve Hispanic students' access to higher education.

Nilsson, Nina L. "How Does Hispanic Portrayal in Children's Books Measure Up after 40 years? The Answer Is 'It Depends.' " *The Reading Teacher* (March 2005): 534–48.

Since 2003, Hispanics have been officially recognized by the U.S. Census Bureau as the largest minority group in the United States. The article reviews twenty-one primary studies of Hispanic literature and presents a comparison of the studies in chart format. The results suggest that progress has been made in some areas but that there is still much work to be done. The article includes Internet addresses for references, Hispanic literature awards, and list of good Hispanic and multicultural literature.

# Resources

## Books

*Student Almanac of Hispanic American History.* 3 vols. Greenwood, 2003. ISBN 0-313-32605-3 Middle School

*UXL Hispanic American Reference Library: Almanac, Biography, Chronology, Voices.* 4 vols. UXL, 2002. ISBN 0-7876-6602-5

## Organizations

Association for the Advancement of Mexican-Americans
6001 Gulf Freeway, Building B-1, Suite 102
Houston, Texas, TX 77023
(713) 926-5464

Congressional Hispanic Caucus Institute
504 C Street NE
Washington, D.C. 20002
(202) 543-1771/(800) EXCEL DC
http://wwwchci.org

Cuban American National Council
1223 SW 4 Street
Miami, Fl 33135
(305) 642-3484
http://www.cnc.org

Hands Across Cultures
P.O. Box 2215
Espanola, NM 87532
(505) 747-1889
http://www.la-tierra.com/hacc

Hispanic Council on International Relations
1111 19 Street, NW, Suite 1000
Washington, D.C. 20036
(202) 776-1754
http://www.hcir.org

## Web Sites

**Annotated Bibliography of Children's Literature focusing on Latino people, history, and culture:** http://clnet.ucla.edu/Latino_Bibliography.html

**Hispanic online.com:** http://www.hispaniconline.com

**Mapping census 2000: The Geography of U.S. Diversity:** http://www.census.gov/population/www/cen2000/atlas

**White House Initiative on Educational Excellence for Hispanic Americans:** http://yesican.gov

# Awards

## Americas Award for Children's and Young Adult Literature

This award was established in 1993. Two awards are given, one primary and one secondary, in recognition of U.S. Published works of fiction, poetry, folklore, or selected nonfiction that authentically and engagingly portray Latin America, the Caribbean, or Latinos in the U.S. See http://www.uwm.edu/Dept/CLACS/outreach/americas.html.

### *Americas Award Winner 2005*

Herrera, Juan Felipe. *Cinnamon Girl: Letters Found Inside a Cereal Box.* 2005

### *American Award Honorable Mentions*

Hanson, Regina. *A Season for Mangoes.* 2005.

Canales, Viola. *The Tequila Worm.* 2005

## Pura Belpre Award

This award was founded in 1996 and is sponsored by the Association for Library Service to Children and the National Association to Promote Library service to Speakers of Spanish. This award is given every two years to honor Latino writers and illustrators whose work celebrates the Latino cultural experience in a work of literature for youth.

### *2006 Award Winners*

**For Narrative:** Viola Canales. *The Tequila Worm.*
**For Illustration:** Raul Colon. *Dona Flor: A Tall Tale about a Giant Woman with a Great Big Heart.*
**Honor Books for Narrative:**

Carmen T. Bernier-Grand. *Cesar: Si, Se Puede! Yes, We Can!*

Mora, Pat. *Dona Flor: A Tall Tale about a Giant Woman with a Great Big Heart.*

Ryan, Pam Muñoz. *Becoming Naomi León.* 2005

**Honor Books for Illustration**

Delacre, Lulu (selected and illustrated by). *Arrorró Mi Niño: Latino Lullabies and Gentle Games.*

Diaz, David. *Cesar: Si, Se Puede! Yes, We Can!*

Lopez, David, Illustrator. *My Name Is Celia: The Life of Celia Cruz/Me Llamo Celia: Vida de Celia Cruz.* Written by Monica Brown.

## Tomas Rivera Mexican American Children's Book Award

This award was established in 1955 by Texas State University to encourage "authors, illustrators and publishers of books that authentically reflect the lives of Mexican American children and young adults in the United States." One book a year is chosen. The award is named for Tomas Rivera, who grew up as a migrant farm worker and became chancellor of the University of California at Riverside. Both fiction and nonfiction books are eligible. See http://www.ci.austin.tx.us/library/youth_rive.htm

### *2004 Winner*

Ryan, Pam Muñoz. *Becoming Naomi León.*

# Chapter 8

# Middle East

## Introduction

The definition of the Middle East encompasses a vast area including Israel. Since Israel does not share the same religion or background, we have kept it separate in this chapter so that the individual books will be more easily recognized.

Middle Easterners are one of the fastest-growing immigrant groups in the United States. In three decades, the population has increased from 200,000 in 1970 to nearly 1.5 million in 2000. Of these, about 150,000 or 10 percent are illegal aliens. In this same time period, the numbers of Middle Easterners who are now Muslim have increased from 15 percent to 73 percent in 2000. The number of non-Muslims has increased also, just not as fast.

Interest in immigrating to the United States is still high after September 11, but there is greater scrutiny of new applications and some fear of recrimination or anti–Middle East sentiment.

## Definition

**Middle East; also called Mideast:** (loosely) The area from Libya east to Afghanistan, usually including Egypt, Sudan, Israel, Jordan, Lebanon, Syria, Turkey, Iraq, Iran, Saudi Arabia, and the other countries of the Arabian peninsula. (http://www.dictionary.com)

# Annotations

Abdu, Rashid. *Journey of a Yemeni Boy.* Dorrance, 2005. ISBN 0-9059-6711-7 Adult

Rashid left his small village when he was nine, and "although I left Yemen many years ago when still a child, Yemen never left me. Those early years in the village had a profound influence on my life and gave me a sense of purpose." Rashid was asked to stay with his five-year-old cousin who was ill with yellow fever. While there, Rashid became obsessed with the idea of going to school and becoming a doctor. From then on, getting a job, learning English, going to school, and becoming a doctor would be his driving force and influence his life decisions. Against much opposition from his family, Rashid spent his teen years in the United States and fulfilled his dreams of becoming a doctor and surgeon. In his village, money was most important; it took care of the necessities of life. "To share dreams, which took years to materialize like going to study medicine, with people whose dreams were confined to the next meal, was meaningless." Presently Dr. Abdu is Emeritus Director of Surgical Education at the St. Elizabeth Health Center and Professor Emeritus of Surgery, Northwestern Ohio Universities College of Medicine.

Budhos, Marina. *Ask Me No Questions.* Atheneum Books for Young Readers, 2006. ISBN 1-4169-0351-8 Gr. 7–10

Nadira and her talented older sister, Aisha, were always told to blend in at school and be careful about what they said about their family. Nadira's family are illegal immigrants. They have lived on expired visas for eight years in New York City. Prior to September 11, immigrants filled a need, and Immigration allowed them to stay. Nadira's father, Abba, has applied for residency and worked with several lawyers, with no positive results. After September 11, Muslims are rounded up, detained, questioned, and, in some cases, deported. Abba does not know what to do, but he decides to take the family to the Canadian border and ask for asylum. His request is turned down, Abba is detained at the border, questioned, and put in jail because of his contributions to a religious organization. Nadira and Aisha are sent back to New York City to continue school and wait patiently to see what Immigration would do. Aisha's world, of always being the smart daughter and possible valedictorian, begins to crumble as she fears that she will be deported at any minute. It is up to Nadira, the slow and patient daughter, to figure out that Abba is a victim of mistaken identity and that the judge needs to look at this Muslim family in a different way and give them one more chance to have their residency status changed.

Nagda, Ann Whitehead. *Dear Whiskers.* Scholastic, 2000. ISBN 0-8234-1495-7 Gr. 2–4

Jenny is in fourth grade, and her class is learning how to write letters. Jenny is writing to a second-grade girl at her school named, Sameera, and she is pretending to be Whiskers, a mouse who lives in Sameera's desk. All of the other students received letters from their pen pals, but Sameera replied, "No Mouse in desk?" Jenny feels awful, and when she did not receive a second response from Sameera, her teacher sends her down to the second grade, where she meets Sameera. Jenny attempts to read to Sameera, and once gets her to smile. Jenny wishes that her pen pal would be like everyone else who reads and speaks English. She learns that Sameera is a new student from Saudi Arabia. Jenny perseveres and thinks of a way to show Sameera that she wants to help her and make writing letters fun. At the same time, Jenny learns about Sameera's culture.

# Bibliography

Hingoro, Samira. *A Marriage Proposal.* Faith, 2003. ISBN 0-9743167-0-9 Young Adult

Ismail, Suzy. *The BFF Sisters: Jennah's New Friends.* Amana, 2001. ISBN 1-59008-005-X Juvenile

Khan, Rukhsana. *Dahling, If You LUV Me, Would You Please, Please Smile.* Turtleback Books, 1999. ISBN 0-606-20472-5 Gr. 7–9

Lipp, Frederick. *Fatima.* Mondo, 2006. ISBN 1-59336-302-4 Juvenile

Mobin-Uddin, Asma. *My Name Is Bilal.* Boyds Mills, 2001. ISBN 1-59078-175-9 Gr. 3–6

Nye, Naomi Shihab. *Habibi.* Simon & Schuster, 1997. ISBN 0-689-80149-1 Gr. 5–8

Stine, Catherine. *Refugees.* Random House, 2006. ISBN 0-385-90216-6 Young Adult

## Picture Books

Brown, Tricia. *Salaam: A Muslim American Boy's Story.* Henry Holt, 2006. ISBN 0-8050-6538-1 Juvenile

English, Karen. *Nadia's Hands.* Boyds Mills, 2003. ISBN 1-56397-667-6 Gr. K–3

Matze, Claire Sidhom. *The Stars in My Geddoh's Sky.* Albert Whitman, 1999. ISBN 0-8075-5332-8 Gr. 0–3

Morris, Ann. *Grandma Hekmatt Remembers: An Arab-American Family Story.* Lerner Group, 2003. ISBN 0-7613-2864-5 Gr. 2–4

Nye, Naomi Shihab. *Sitti's Secrets.* Center for Applied Research in Education, 1998. ISBN 0-87628-371-7 Gr. K–3

## Nonfiction

Anderson, Marilyn D. *Arab Americans.* Gareth Stevens, 2006. ISBN 0-8368-7307-6 Juvenile

Beshir, Ekram, and Mohamed Rida Beshir. *Muslim Teens: Today's Worry, Tomorrow's Hope: A Pratical Islamic Parenting Guide.* Amana, 2001. ISBN 1-59008-004-1 Adult

Beshir, Sumaiya. *Everyday Struggles: The Stories of Muslim Teens.* Amana, 2004. ISBN 1-59008-030-0 Juvenile

Demi. *Muhammad.* Simon & Schuster, 2003. ISBN 0-689-85264-9 Gr. 2–5

Egendorf, Laura K. *Islam in America.* Thomson Gale, 2005. ISBN 0-7377-2728-4 Gr. 10–12

Esposito, John L. *What Everyone Needs to Know About Islam.* Oxford University Press, 2002. ISBN0-19-515713-3 General Adult

Gulevich, Tanya. *Understanding Islam and Muslim Traditions.* Omnigraphics, 2004. ISBN 0-7808-0704-9 General Adult

Hasan, Asma Gull. *American Muslims: The New Generation.* Continuum, 2001. ISBN 0-8264-1362-5 General Adult

_____. *Why I Am a Muslim: An American Odyssey.* Thorsons/Element Books, 2005. ISBN 0-00-717534-5 Young Adult

Haskins, James. *Count Your Way Through the Arab World.* Sagebrush Education Resources, 1991. ISBN 0-613-68224-6 Gr. 3–6

Hoyt-Goldsmith, Diane. *Celebrating Ramadan.* Holiday House. 2005. ISBN 0-8234-1762-X Gr. 4–6

Johnson, Julia. *A Is for Arabia.* Stacey International, 2004. ISBN 1-900988-55-0 Gr. 2-5

Khan, Aisha Karen. *What You Will See Inside a Mosque.* Skylight Paths, 2003. ISBN 1-893361-60-8 Gr. 1–5

Khan, Rukhsana. *Muslim Child: Understanding Islam Through Stories and Poems.* Albert Whitman, 2002. ISBN 0-8075-5307-7 Gr. 3–7

Macaulay, David. *Mosque.* Houghton Mifflin, 2003. ISBN 0-618-24034-9 Gr. 5 & up

Morris, Neil. *The Atlas of Islam: People, Daily Life, and Traditions.* Baron's Educational, 2003. ISBN 0-7641-5631-4 Gr. 5–8

Naidoo, Beverly. *Out of Bounds: Seven Stories of Conflict and Hope.* HarperCollins, 2003. ISBN 0-06-050799-3 Gr. 5–7

Nasr, Seyyed Hossein. *A Young Muslim's Guide to the Modern World.* Kazi, 1994. ISBN 1-56744-476-8 Gr. 7–12

Nye, Naomi Shihab. *19 Varieties of Gazelle: Poems of the Middle East.* Greenwillow, 2002. ISBN 0-06-009765-5 Young Adult

Sears, Evelyn. *Muslims and the West.* Mason Crest, 2003. ISBN 1-59084-700-8 Young Adult

Stotsky, Sandra *The Arab Americans.* Chelsea House, 1999. ISBN 0-7910-5051-3 Gr. 4–7

Wachal, Barbara S. *The American Encounter with Islam.* Mason Crest, 2004. ISBN 1-59084-699-0 Young Adult

Wilkinson, Philip, et al. *Islam.* DK, 2005. ISBN 0-7566-1078-8 Gr. PS–7

Wolf, Bernard. *Coming to America: A Muslim Story.* Lee & Low, 2003. ISBN 1-58430-086-8 Gr. 0–8

Wormser, Richard. *American Islam: Growing Up Muslim in America.* DIANE, 2004. ISBN 0-7567-8423-9 Gr. 6–9

## Series

*Creation of the Modern Middle East.* Chelsea House. ISBN 0-7910-6503-0

*Introducing Islam.* 8 vols. Mason Crest. ISBN 1-59084-696-6 Gr. 6 & up

# Discussion Questions

- Since September 11, are Middle Eastern people looked upon differently?

- Do you have a good, clear understanding of the Muslim religion? Way of life?

- What is the level of acceptance for traditional Middle Eastern clothing?

- Are fellow students more accepting because we see Middle Eastern people more often?

# Featured Author

## Khan, Rukhsana

**Birthplace:** Lahore, Pakistan
**Date of Birth:** March 13, 1962
**Current Home:** Toronto, Canada
**Titles**

*Silly Chicken* (2005)

*Ruler of the Courtyard* (2003)

*Dahling, If You Luv Me Would You Please, Please Smile* (1999)

*Muslim Child* (1999)

*Bedtime Ba-a-a-lk* (1998)

*The Roses in My Carpet* (1998)

**Interesting Information**

- Rukhsana immigrated to Canada when she was three.

- Rukhsana and her family were persecuted from day one because they were different.

- In eighth grade, her teacher told her she was a writer.

- At first, she thought only white people could be writers, but "I'd love to be able to write the stories that I love to read."

**Web Site:** http://www.rukhsanakhan.com

**E-mail:** rukhsana@rukhsanakhan.com

# Annotated Journal Article

Al-Hazzd, Tami. "Arab Children's Literature: An Update." *Book Links* (January 2006): 11–17.
    The article indicates that Arabs represent seventeen different countries. Not all Arabs are Muslims (only about 20 percent of the world's Muslim population is Arab). Unfortunately, there is much incorrect information about Arabs being circulated. This article features annotated picture

books, novels, story collections, poetry, folktales, and nonfiction titles that accurately reflect Arab culture, heritage, and people.

# Resources

## Books

Hasan, Asma Gull. *American Muslims: The New Generation.* Continuum International, 2002 ISBN 0826414168

Ruthven, Malise, and Azim Nanji. *Historical Atlas of Islam.* Harvard University Press, 2004. ISBN 0-674001385-9

Sarroub, Loukia K. *All American Yemeni Girls: Being Muslim in a Public School.* University of Pennsylvania Press, 2005. ISBN 0-812-23833-8

*UXL Arab American Reference Library: Almanac, Biography, Voices.* 4 vols. UXL, 1999. ISBN 0-7876-2957-X

## Organization

American-Arab Anti-Discrimination Committee
4201 Connecticut Ave. NW. #300
Washington, DC 20008
(202) 244-2990
www.adc.org

## Web Sites

**Children's Book with Muslim and Related Cultural Themes:** http://rukhsanakhan.com/muslimbooks.htm

**Islam—Empire of Faith:** http://www.pbs.org/empires/islam

**Meet Sa'id. Amd Arab Teenager:** http://www.amideast.org/offices/Kuwait.Saud/default.htm

**On the Line: Islam:** http://www.orfam.org/uk/coolplanet/onthe line/explore/journey/algeria/islam

**An Open Door to the Arab World:** http://www.al-bab.com/ (Brian Whitaker, editor of the British Newspaper, the *Guardian,* developed this Web site to introduce non-Arabs to the Arabs and their culture.)

# Award

## Middle East Book Award

Established in 1981, the Middle East Outreach Council (MEOC) is a national nonprofit organization working to increase public knowledge about the peoples places, and cultures of the Middle East, including the Arab world, Israel, Iran, Turkey, and Afghanistan. In 1999, it established the Middle East Book Award for picture books, literature for children or young adults, and reference books for youth that accurately portray and contribute to the understanding of the Middle East.

## 2005 Middle East Book Awards

### Picture Book

Stamaty, Mark Alan. *Alia's Mission: Saving the Books of Iraq.*

### Honor Books

Winter, Jeanette. *The Librarian of Basra.*

Shulevitz, Uri. *The Travels of Benjamin of Tudela.*

### Youth Literature

Marston, Elsa. *Figs and Fate.*

# Introduction: Judaism

Judaism is not only a religion but also a way of life. Modern Jews generally belong to one of three groups "people who practice Judaism and have a Jewish ethnic background (sometimes including those who do not have strictly matrilineal descent), people without Jewish parents who have converted to Judaism, and those Jews who, while not practicing Judaism as a religion, still identify themselves as Jewish by virtue of their family's Jewish descent and their own cultural and historical identification with the Jewish people." (Wikipedia) There are 13 million Jews worldwide and almost 6 million in the United States.

# Definition

**Jewish:** Of or relating to the Jews or their culture or religion. (Magazine Publishers of America)

# Annotations

*Jewish Humor Stories for Kids.* Pitspopany Press, 1998. ISBN 0-943706-77-7 Gr. 5–8
    This book is the result of a contest by American Jewish Librarians for the best short humorous stories. The stories had to be Jewish, for kids, and by nonpublished authors. The first-place winner was *Breakfast without Bagels.* Jeff Kinder is sixteen, and his younger brother is eleven. Their family has just moved to a town in Michigan that has no bagel store. There are no other Jewish families living in Hillside, where his father has just started a new job that includes dressing up and playing Santa Claus for the town. Their lives become complicated when they receive the news that their Uncle Yoav is coming for a visit all the way from Israel. Each family member decides to tell their employer, friends, and classmates about their uncle and that they themselves are Jewish, with surprising results.

Cohen, Barbara. *Molly's Pilgrim.* HarperCollins, 1998. ISBN 0-688-16279-7 Gr. 1–4

> Molly does not like her new school because the girls make fun of her language and her Jewish heritage. Molly has immigrated to the United States from Russia. In November, her class studies Thanksgiving, and everyone is asked to bring in a pilgrim doll. Molly's mother makes a doll that looks just like Molly when she first came to the United States. The children make fun of her doll, so the teacher intervenes and explains that her doll is a modern pilgrim.

Mazer, Norma Fox. *Good Night Maman.* Harcourt Children's Books, 1999. ISBN 0-15-201468-3 Gr. 4–7

> Karin is ten years old and hiding in an attic hidden from the occupying Germans with her brother and mother until they are forced to leave Paris and head south. When Maman becomes ill, Karin and her brother leave her behind and board a refugee ship bound for America in 1944. In the remainder of the novel, Karin and her brother adjust to the loneliness, surviving trauma and life in a refugee camp in Oswego, New York, until they leave to live with their aunt in California.

McDonough, Yona Zeldis. *The Doll with the Yellow Star.* Henry Holt, 2005. ISBN 0-8050-6337-0 Gr. 3–5

> At eight years old, Claudine is forced to wear a yellow star on her coat, so she sews a yellow star on the inside of her doll's cape. When her parents tell her that by a miracle they have arranged for her to leave France for America, Claudine insists that she take her favorite doll. Claudine arrives in New York without her doll because as they were docking, the ship catches fire, and she is not allowed back in her cabin. At the end of World War II, her father arrives, thin and frail, and Claudine realizes that Maman will not be coming back. Claudine and her father establish a home in Brooklyn in a new land that offers them a safe home. They furnish their home with item from auctions, and one day her father buys her a chest in which to keep her blankets. When they explore the contents, Claudine realizes that her much loved doll has been restored.

\_\_\_\_\_. *Hammerin' Hank: The Life of Hank Greenberg.* Walker & Company, 2006. ISBN 0-8027-8997-8 Gr. 2–5

> Hammerin' Hank was not the first Jewish ball player in the history of the game, but he was the most famous at the time. The game did not come easily to Hank Greenberg; he had to work at it. He played for the Detroit Tigers, but people resented the fact that he was a rising star and they called him names, showing their anti-Semitism. But to the Jews of America, Hammerin' Hank was a hero.

Weidt, Maryann N. *Oh, the Places He Went.* Carolrhoda Books, 1994. ISBN 0-87614-627-2 Gr. 3–6

> This is a biography of Theodor Seuss Geisel, a unique artist whose high school teacher encouraged him to try a career other than art. His career takes off when he creates an ad for Flit insect repellant. When he wrote his first book, *And to Think I Saw It on Mulberry Street,* he discovered his love of writing for children. Dr. Seuss worked into his late eighties, and the best slogan he could think of to leave with the United States was, "We can do and we've got to do better than this."

# Bibliography

*Always Remember Me: How One Family Survived World War II.* Athenuem Books for Young Readers. ISBN 0-689-86920-7 Gr. 2–6

Asher, Sandy. *With All My Heart, with All My Mind: Thirteen Stories About Growing Up Jewish.* DIANE, 2004. ISBN 0-7567-7692-9 Gr. 4–8

Avrech, Robert J. *The Hebrew Kid and the Apache Maiden.* Seraphic Press, 2005. ISBN 0975438212 Gr. 5–7

Blume, Judy. *Are You There God? It's Me, Margaret.* Book Wholesalers, 2002. ISBN 0-7587-9131-3 Gr, 5–7

Codell, Esme Raji. *Hanukkah, Shmanukkah!* Hyperion Books for Children, 2005. ISBN 0-7868-5179-1 Gr. 3–5

Cohn, Janice. *The Christmas Menorahs: How a Town Fought Hate.* Albert Whitman, 2004. ISBN 0-8075-1153-6 Gr. 3–5

Glaser, Linda. *Bridge to America: Based on a True Story.* Houghton Mifflin, 2005. ISBN 0-618-56301-6 Gr. 4–7

Lasky, Kathryn. *Broken Song.* Viking, 2005. ISBN 0670059315 Gr. 5–9

Meyer, Carolyn. *Drummers of Jericho.* Harcourt Children's Books, 1995. ISBN 0-15-200190-5 Gr. 5–9

Miklowitz, Gloria D. *The Enemy Has a Face.* William B. Eerdmans, 2004. ISBN 0-8028-5261-8 Gr. 9 & up

Napoli, Donna Jo. *The King of Mulberry Street.* Random House. ISBN 0-385-74653-9 Gr. 5–8

Nislick, June Levitt. *Zayda Was a Cowboy.* Jewish Publication Society, 2005. ISBN 0-8276-0817-9 Gr. 4–7

Sachs, Marilyn. *Call Me Ruth.* HarperTrophy, 1995. ISBN 0-688-13737-7 Gr. 4–7

_____. *Lost in America.* Roaring Brook Press, 2005. ISBN 1-596643-040-0 Gr. 5 & up

Schwabach, Karen. *A Pickpocket's Tale.* Random House, 2006. ISBN 0-375-93379-0 Gr. 3–7

Stein, Tamar. *Light Years.* Knopf, 2005. ISBN 0-375-83023-5 Gr. 9 & up

Tal, Eve. *Double Crossing: A Jewish Immigration Story.* Cinco Puntos Press, 2005. ISBN 0-938317-94-6 Gr. 3–7

## Picture Books

Blanc, Esther Silverstein. *Berchick.* Volcano Press, 1989. ISBN 0-912078-81-2 Gr. 0–5

Jacobs, Laurie. *A Box of Candles.* Boyds Mills, 2005. ISBN 1590781694 Gr. 1–4

Polacco, Patricia. *Keeping Quilt.* Simon & Schuster, 2001. ISBN 0-689-84447-6 Gr. PS–3

Rael, Elsa Okon. *Rivka's First Thanksgiving.* Simon & Schuster, 2001. ISBN 0-689-83901-4 Gr. PS–2

## Nonfiction

Adelman, Penina, Ali Feldman, and Shulamit Reinharz. *The JGirls Guide: The Young Jewish Woman's Handbook for Coming of Age.* Jewish Lights, 2005. ISBN 1-58023-215-9 Juvenile

Brooks, Philip. *Extraordinary Jewish Americans.* Children's Press, 1998. ISBN 0-516-20609-5 Gr. 6 & up

Canfield, Jack. *Chicken Soup for the Jewish Soul.* Health Communications, 2001. ISBN 1-55874-899-7 General Adult

Moore, H.S. *Liberty's Poet: Emma Lazarus.* TurnKey Press, 2005. ISBN 0-9754803-4-0 Gr. 7–9

Streissguth, Thomas. *Say It with Music: A Story About Irving Berlin.* Carolrhoda Books, 1994. ISBN 0-87614-810-0 Gr. 3–6

# Discussion Questions

- Do the experiences of the author adequately prepare him or her to write this story?
- Why are authors not writing about modern Jewish children?
- Does the dialogue accurately reflect the speech of the people and the time period?
- Are the characters real and authentic? Do you know anyone like the characters in the book?

# Featured Author

## Donna Jo Napoli

**Birthplace:** Miami, Florida
**Date of Birth:** February 28, 1948
**Current Home:** Swarthmore, Pennsylvania
**Titles**

*Sly the Sleuth and the Food Mysteries* (2007, with son Robert)

*Bobby the Bold* (2006, with daughter Eva)

*Fire in the Hills* (2006)

*North* (2006)

*Sly the Sleuth and the Sports Mysteries* (2006, with son Robert)

*Ugly* (2006)

*Albert* (2005)

*Beast* (2005)

*Bound* (2005)

*Breath* (2005)

*The Great God Plan* (2005)

*The King of Mulberry Street* (2005)

*Pink Magic* (2005)

*Sly the Sleuth and the Pet Mysteries* (2005, with son Robert)

*Zel* (2005)

*Gracie: The Pixie of the Puddle* (2004)

*Hotel Jungle* (2004)

*Song of the Magdalene* (2004)

*Daughter of Venice* (2003)

*Three Days* (2003)

*Flamingo Dream* (2002)

*Albert* (2001)

*Crazy Jack* (2001)

*Hang in There* (2001)

*How Hungry Are You?* (2001)

*Partners* (2001)

*Spinners* (2001)

*April Flowers* (2000)

*Changing Tunes* (2000)

*For the Love of Venice* (2000)

*Give and Take* (2000)

*Happy Holidays* (2000)

*Know-It-All* (2000)

*Left Out* (2000)

*Lies and Lemons* (2000)

*New Voices* (2000)

*No Fair!* (2000)

*Running Away* (2000)

*Shelley Shock* (2000)

*Sirena* (2000)

*Stones in the Water* (1999)

## Interesting Information

- Napoli writes a variety of books, from professional books related to her expertise in linguistics, to fiction, to picture books, to works for young adults.

- Her books have been translated into Chinese, Danish, Dutch, Farsi, German, Hebrew, Italian, Japanese, Korean, Portuguese, and Spanish; they will soon be translated into Thai.

- She has five children and has coauthored books with two of them, Robert Furrow and Elena Furrow.

**Web Site:** http://www.donnajonapoli.com/

**Contact:**
Donna Jo Napoli
226 Park Ave, Swarthmore, PA 19081
(610) 328-6558 or (610) 328-8422
E-mail: dnapoli1@swarthmore.edu

# Annotated Journal Article

Cummins, June. "Rivka's Way / Dave at Night / Stolen Words." *Melus* (July 1, 2003): 237.
    Jewish children's literature was defined by Sydneys Taylor's All-of-a-Kind Family books published from the 1950s through the 1970s. Today it is difficult to identify Jewish Children's Literature. The books that feature Jewish children are for the most part historical fiction that includes children who have immigrated or whose parents immigrated, Holocaust narratives, and, in rare cases, books featuring a contemporary American Jewish child. One might conclude that the modern Jewish child does not experience any Jewish or non-Jewish issues. The author focuses on three titles, one from each category, and comes to the conclusion that "Jews are still not fully integrated into American society" and the type of books written today reflects this fact.

# Resources

## Books

Chametzky, Jules. *Jewish American Literature: A Norton Anthology.* W. W. Norton & Company, 2000. ISBN 0-393-04809-8

## Organizations

American Jewish Committee
The Jacob Blaustein Building
165 East 56th Street
New York, NY 10022-2746
Phone (212) 751-4000
http://ajc.org

Anti-Defamation League
823 United Nations Plaza
New York, NY 10017
Phone (212) 490-2525
www.adl.org

## Web Sites

**American Jewish Committee:** http://www.ajc.org/site/c.ijITI2PHKoG/b.685761/k.CB97/Home.htm

**American Jewish Congress:** http://www.ajcongress.org/

**International Fellowship of Christians and Jews:** http://www.ifcj.org/site/PageServer

**Jewish Defense League:** http://www.ifcj.org/site/PageServer

# Awards

## The Sydney Taylor Book Award

The Sydney Taylor Book Award represents the best in Jewish Literature that authentically portrays the Jewish experience.

### *2006 Award for Younger Readers*

Silverman, Erica. *Sholom's Treasure: How Sholom Aleichem Became a Writer*

### *Honor Books for Younger Readers*

Borden, Louise. *The Journey that Saved Curious George: The True Wartime Escape of Margaret and H. A. Rey*

Marzollo, Jean. *Ruth and Naomi: A Bible Story*

Olswanger, Anna. *Shlemiel Crooks*

Taback, Simms. *Kibitzers and Fools: Tales My Zayda Told Me*

### *2006 Award for Older Readers*

Littman, Sarah. *Confessions of a Closet Catholic*

### *Honor Books for Older Readers*

Krinitz, Esther Nisenthal, and Bernice Steinhardt. *Memories of Survival*

Napoli, Donna Jo. *The King of Mulberry Street*

Rahlens, Holly-Jane. *Prince William, Maximilian Minsky and Me*

Shulevitz, Uri. *The Travels of Benjamin of Tudela*

# Chapter 9

# Native American/First Nation/North American Indigenous

## Introduction

By the nineteenth century, Native Americans had been pushed onto reservations, areas that were generally poor in resources and isolated from the rest of the country. Young Native Americans were sent away to school to Americanize them and introduce them to a new way of life. In the process, they were not allowed to do, say, think, or dress like Native Americans. They were cut off from everything they knew. Today there are more than 562 distinct tribes, and Native Americans reside in every state. Native Americans moved to the cities for good jobs, education, and entertainment. Native Americans still face issues of discrimination, health, and education.

There has been an increase in the population from 350,000 in 1920 to more than 2.5 million today. There are several reasons for this. One is an increase in cultural pride, and the other is the casinos the Native Americans have begun to build on their reservations. The Social Science Research Network (2002; http://www.ssrn.com) states that four years after tribes opened casinos, employment increased by 26 percent and tribal population by 12 percent. Many young adults moved back to the reservations for jobs. In spite of this, unemployment, diabetes, heart disease, and suicide are high.

# Definition

**American Indian and Alaska Native:** A person having origins in any of the original peoples of North and South America (including Central America), and who maintains tribal affiliation or community attachment. (Magazine Publishers of America)

# Annotations

Aveni, Anthony. *The First Americans: The Story of Where They Came from and Who They Became.* Scholastic, 2005. ISBN 0-439-55144-7 Gr. 4–6

The first migration began 20,000 years ago when there was a land bridge between North America and Asia. After the climate changed and the land bridge disappeared, what was left were the ancestors of what was to become the various American Indian groups. Chapters include information about the Tainos, the Woodland Peoples, the Ohio Moundbuilders, the Anasazi, natives of the northwest Coast, and the Timucua, all of whom were descendants of the first migration.

Brown, Don. *Jim Thorpe: Bright Path.* Roaring Brook Press, 2006. ISBN 1-59643-041-9 Gr. 2–4

A picture book introduction to Jim Thorpe whose Indian name means "Bright Path." He was raised on the Oklahoma plains, and by the age of ten, he could lasso a wild horse. When he was six, Jim was sent to a school for Indian children where he was to learn the ways of the white man. "Jim did not like it and often ray away." This continued, so his father just sent him to a similar school but farther away in Carlisle, Pennsylvania. One day at the new school, the track team was practicing, and Jim asked if he could try the high jump. Jim, in regular street clothes, cleared the bar on his first try, breaking the school's high-jump record. This was just the beginning; Jim went on to participate in the fifth Olympic Games in 1912. He won the pentathlon with a score that has never been equaled; three days later, he won the more grueling decathlon. " 'You are the greatest athlete in the world,' the king of Sweden declared as he presented Jim with an Olympic gold medal."

Bruchac, Joseph. *Code Talker: A Novel About the Navajo Marines of World War Two.* Dial for Young Readers, 2005. ISBN 0-8037-2921-9 Gr. 5 & up

At an early age, Joe is chosen to leave his family and go to school to learn the ways and language of the white man. In the process, his long hair is cut, his Navajo clothes and decorations are taken away, and he is forbidden to use his native language. Joe is able to adjust more easily than other Native Americans, and soon he surprises his teachers with his intelligence. When he is fifteen years old, the Japanese bomb Pearl Harbor, and the Native Americans are actively recruited. Joe enlists in the Marines and is asked to participate in a secret operation. Much to his surprise, his ability to communicate in both English and Navajo is prized and encouraged. After a few weeks of training, Joe is sent to the Pacific as a Navajo code talker. He is only seventeen years old, yet he is in the middle of a war with many adventures ahead.

_____. *The Journal of Jesse Smoke: A Cherokee Boy: Trail of Tears, 1838.* Scholastic, 2001. ISBN 0-439-12197-3 Gr. 4–8

It is 1838, and the Cherokee Nation has been reduced to a small portion of the place where Georgia, Tennessee, and North Carolina come together. Now the U.S. government wants to move these hardworking and industrious people west of the Mississippi. This is Jesse Smoke's diary of events leading up to and during the Cherokees' forced removal to Oklahoma, a journey known as the Trail of Tears that caused the death of one-fourth of the tribe's people.

Carvell, Marlene. *Sweetgrass Basket.* Dutton Children's Books, 2005. ISBN 0-525- 47547-8 Gr. 5–8

Mattie and Sarah promise their father that they will be good when they are sent to the Carlisle Indian Industrial School. He is convinced that this will be the best thing for them. The unhappy children tell, in alternating chapters, how their lives have changed as the move from a warm and loving home to one of fear and sorrow. All of the children at the school are encouraged to tell on each other, punished for minor infractions, and have given up all remembrances, clothing, and speech of their Native American cultures. Mattie is falsely accused of stealing the head mistress' pin. She is publicly humiliated and beaten. Mattie runs away with nowhere to go because she is ashamed and does not want to disappoint her father. This compelling story is told in prose and is based on the family of the author's husband.

_____. *Who Will Tell My Brother?* Hyperion Books for Children, 2004. ISBN 0-7868-1657 0 Gr. 7 & up

In verse form, this is the story of Evan and his struggle to make a difference and come to terms with who he is. In his senior year of high school, Evan petitions the school board to change their mascot and some of the traditions that show disrespect to the Indian Nation. He learns that it is one thing to ask to remove a picture of an Indian, but it is another thing to ask for a change in attitude. Although Evan does not look like an Indian, he knows it is not how one looks that is important but how one feels. When his petition is turned down, a fellow student brags that his side has won and Evan has lost. Evan replies, "No … we've all lost."

Dennis, Yvonne Wakim, and Arlene Hirschfelder. *Children of Native America Today.* Charlesbridge, 2003. ISBN 1-57091-499-0 Gr. 2–5

This book includes a few of the more than five hundred native cultures, native peoples of Alaska and Hawaii, small and large nations, and confederations made up of several tribes. It has many pictures, with a short overview of what they are like today and a sidebar of quick facts.

Erdrich, Louise. *Game of Silence.* HarperCollins, 2006. ISBN 0-06-441029-3 Gr. 5–8

Omakayas lives on an island in Lake Superior. Her life was ever changing; her Ojibwa tribe built birchbark houses in the summer, went to gather rice in the fall, and lived in their cedar log cabin near a town in the winter. The greatest change may soon affect them all. The chimookomanag or white people would force them to move west, away from all that they have ever known.

Mikaelsen, Ben. *Touching Spirit Bear.* HarperCollins, 2001. ISBN 0-380-97744-3 Gr. 5–6

Cole Matthews is a bully with so much anger inside that he viciously beats a ninth-grade classmate—a beating so brutal it results in brain damage. Cole faces a prison sentence but is offered an alternative: Circle Justice. He is happy to take this opportunity instead of prison because he still blames everyone but himself for the things that happen and feels that this will be much easier than serving time in prison. Circle Justice is based on Native American tradition, and Cole is banished, alone, to a remote Alaskan island for a year. Cole has an encounter with a Spirit Bear and is badly mauled and left for dead. After finally being rescued, he spends six months recovering from his injuries. During that time, he realizes he must control his anger and change his ways.

# Bibliography

Belarde-Lewis, Miranda. *Meet Lydia: A Native Girl from Southeast Alaska.* NMAI with Council Oak Books, 2004. ISBN 1-57178-147-1 Juvenile

Bruchac, Joseph. *Eagle Song.* Dial, 1997. ISBN 0-8037-1918-3 Gr. 2–4

_____. *The Heart of a Chief.* Dial, 1998. ISBN 0-803702276-1 Gr. 5–8

_____. *Hidden Roots.* Scholastic, 2006. ISBN 0-439-35359-9 Gr. 5–9

_____. *The Warriors.* Darby Creek, 2004. ISBN 1-58196-002-6 Gr. 5–8

Carlson, Lori Marie, ed. *Moccasin Thunder: American Indian Stories for Today.* HarperCollins, 2005. ISBN 0-06-623957-5 Gr. 9 & up

Davidson, A. L. *The Spirit Line.* Penguin Group, 2004. ISBN 0-670-03645-5 Young Adult

Dorris, Michael. *The Window.* Hyperion, 1997. ISBN 0-7868-1373-3 Gr. 6–9

_____. *A Yellow Raft in Blue Water: A Novel.* Sagebrush Education Resources, 2003. ISBN 0-613-61151-9 Gr. 7 & up

Ferris, Jeri. *Native American Doctor: The Story of Susan Laflesche Picotte.* Carolrhoda Books, 1991. ISBN 0-87614-548-9 Gr. 4–6

Hesse, Karen. *Aleutian Sparrow.* Simon & Schuster, 2005. ISBN 1–4169-032705 Gr. 7 & up

Hobbs, William. *Far North,* HarperCollins, 2004. ISBN 0-06-054096-6 Gr. 7 & up

Hunter, Sara Hoagland. *The Unbreakable Code.* Northland, 1996. ISBN 0-87358-638-7 Gr. 4–6

King, Sandra. *Shannon.* Lerner, 1998. ISBN 0-8225-9643-1 Gr. 4–6

Left Hand Bull, Jacqueline, and Suzanne Haldane. *Lakota Hoop Dance.* Dutton Children's Books, 1999. ISBN 0-525-45413-6 Gr. 3–6

Maher, Ramona. *Alice Yazzie's Year.* Tricycle Press, 2004. ISBN 1-58246-080-9 Gr. 3–5

Monture, Joel. *Cloudwalker: Contemporary Native American Stories.* Fulcrum, 1996. ISBN 1-55591-225-7 Gr. 4–7

Oughton, Jerrie. *Music from a Place Called Half Moon.* Turtleback Books, 1997. ISBN 0-606-11003-8 Gr. 6–10

Roessel, Monty. *Kinaalda: A Navajo Grows Up.* Sagebrush Education Resources, 1996. ISBN 0-613-76607-5 Gr. 4–7

Rogers, Jean. *Goodbye, My Island.* Graphic Arts Center, 2005. ISBN 0-88240-538-1 Gr. 2 & up

Savageau, Cheryl. *Muskrat Will Be Swimming.* Tilbury House, 2006. ISBN 0-88448-280-4 Gr. 2–6

Smith, Cynthia Leitich. *Indian Shoes.* HarperCollins, 2002. ISBN 0-06-029531-7 Gr. 3–6

Sneve, Virginia Driving Hawk. *When Thunders Spoke.* University of Nebraska Press, 1993. ISBN 0-8032-9220-1 Gr. 3–6

Sterling, Shirley. *My Name Is Seepeetza.* Douglas & McIntyre, 1992. ISBN 0-88899-165-7 Gr. 5–10

Tayac, Gabrielle. *Meet Naiche: A Native Boy from the Chesapeake Bay Area.* National Museum of the American Indian, 2002. ISBN 1-58270-07209 Gr. 3–6

Von Ahnen, Katherine. *Charlie Young Bear.* Roberts Rinehart, 2000. ISBN 1-57098-001-2 Gr. 2–4

## Picture Books

Ancona, George. *Powwow.* Harcourt, 1993. ISBN 0-15-263268-9 Gr. 1–4

Cowley, Joe. *Big Moon Tortilla.* Boyds Mills, 2003. ISBN 1-56397-601-3 Gr. 1–4

Edwardson, Debby Dahl. *Whale Snow.* Charlesbridge, 2004. ISBN 1-57091-496-6 Gr. K–2

Harjo, Joy. *The Good Luck Cat.* Harcourt, 2000. ISBN 0-15-232197-7 Gr. K–2

Hucko, Bruce. *A Rainbow at Night: The World in Words and Pictures by Navajo Children.* Chronicle, 1997. ISBN 0-8118-1294-5 Gr. 1–6

Kirk, Connie Ann. *Sky Dancers.* Lee & Low, 2004. ISBN 1-58430-162-7 Gr. 1–4

McCain, Becky Ray. *Grandmother's Dreamcatcher.* Albert Whitman, 2004. ISBN 0-8075-3032-8 Gr. 0–3

Noel, Michel. *Good for Nothing.* Groundwood Books, 2006. ISBN 0-88899-616-0 Gr. 9 & up

Orona-Ramirez, Kristy. *Kiki's Journey.* Children's Book Press, 2006. ISBN 0-89239-214-2 Juvenile

Roberta, John. *Proud to Be a Blacksheep.* Salina Bookshelf, 2006. ISBN 1-893354-05-9 Juvenile

Salonen, Roxane Beauclair. *First Salmon.* Boyds Mills, 2005. ISBN 1-59078-171-6 Gr. K–3

Santiago, Chiori. *Home to Medicine Mountain.* Children's Book Press, 2002. ISBN 0-89239-176-6 Gr. K–3

Scott, Ann Herbert. *Brave as a Mountain Lion.* Clarion, 1996. ISBN 0-395-66760-7 Gr. 1–4

Secakuku, Susan. *Meet Mindy: A Native Girl from the Southwest.* NMAI with Beyond Words Publishing, 2003. ISBN 1-58270-091-5 Gr. 3–6

Smith, Cynthia Leitich. *Jingle Dancer.* HarperCollins, 2000. ISBN 0-688-16242-8 Gr. PS–5

_____. *Rain Is Not My Indian Name.* Morrow/Avon, 2001. ISBN 0-688-17397-7 Gr. 5–9

Strete, Craig Kee. *The Rattlesnake Who Went to School.* G. P. Putnam's Sons, 2004. ISBN 0-399-23572-8 Gr. PS–K

Waboose, Jan Bourdeau. *Morning on the Lake.* Kids Can Press, 2002. ISBN 1-55074-588-3 Gr. 0–3

## Nonfiction

Allen, Paula Gunn and Patricia Clark Smith. *As Long as the Rivers Flow: The Stories of Nine Native Americans.* Scholastic, 1996. ISBN 0-590-47870-2 Gr. 5–8

Brown, Tricia. *Children of the Native Sun: Young Native Voices of Alaska.* Alaska Northwest, 1998. ISBN 0-88240-500-4 Gr. 2–5

Bruchac, Joseph. *Bowman's Store: A Journey to Myself.* Sagebrush Education Resources, 2001. ISBN 0-613-84717-2 Gr. 7 & up

_____. *Jim Thorpe, Original All-American.* Dial, 2006. ISBN 0-8037-3118-3 Juvenile

Grace, Catherine O'Neill, and Margaret M. Bruchac. *1621: A New Look at Thanksgiving.* National Geographic Society, 2001. ISBN 0-7922-7027-4 Gr. 3–5

Hirschfelder, Arlene B. *Rising Voices: Writings of Young Native Americans.* Ballantine Books, 1993. ISBN 0-8041-1167-7 Gr. 5 & up

Hoyt Goldsmith, Diane. *Arctic Hunter.* Holiday House, 1992. ISBN 0-8234-0972-4 Gr. 3–6

_____. *Buffalo Days.* Holiday House, 1997. ISBN 0-8234-1327-6 Gr. 4–6

_____. *Potlatch: A Tsimshian Celebration.* Holiday House, 1997. ISBN 0-8234-1290-3 Gr. 4–8

Hucko, Bruce. *A Rainbow at Night: The World in Words and Pictures by Navajo Children.* Chronicle, 1997. ISBN 0-8118-1294-4 Gr. 1–6

Kendall, Russ. *Eskimo Boy: Life in an Inupiaq Eskimo Village.* Scholastic, 1994. ISBN 0-590-43695-3 Gr. K–3

Ortiz, Simon. *The People Shall Continue.* Turtleback Books, 1994. ISBN 0-606-06662-4 Gr. 2–6

Peters, Russell M. *Clambake: A Wampanoag Tradition.* Lerner, 1992. ISBN 0-8225-9621-0 Gr. 3-5

Philip, Neil. *In a Sacred Manner I Live: Native American Wisdom.* Clarion, 2005. ISBN 0-618-60483-9 Gr. 5–7

Ross, LaVera. *Grandchildren of the Lakota.* Carolrhoda, 1998. ISBN 1-57505-279-2 Gr. 3–5

Sneve, Virginia Driving Hawk. *Enduring Wisdom: Sayings from Native Americans.* Holiday House, 2005. ISBN 0-8234-1455-8 Gr. 0–3

Tallchief, Maria, and Rosemary Wells. *Tallchief: America's Prima Ballerina.* Viking, 1999. ISBN 0-670-88756-0 Gr. 3–5

## Series

*American Indian Contributions to the World.* Chelsea House

*Contemporaty Native American Issues.* Chelsea House

*First Americans.* Holiday House

*First Peoples Series.* Lerner

*Indian Nations Series.* Steck-Vaughn

*Indians of North America, Heritage Edition.* Chelsea House

Karasch, E. Barrie. *The Library of Intergenerational Learning: Native Americans.* Rosen

*My World: Young Native Americans Today.* Beyond Worlds

*Native Americans.* ABDO

*We Are Still Here: Native American Today.* Lerner

# Discussion Questions

- How influenced are we by the stereotype of Native Americans portrayed in the movies?
- Are Native Americans who live on reservations now integrated into our present culture?
- Do we understand the differences between mainstream Americans and Native Americans?
- Do we have a responsibility to Native Americans today?

# Featured Author

## Joseph Bruchac

**Birthplace:** October 16, 1942
**Date of Birth:** Saratoga Springs, New York
**Current Home:** Greenfield Center, New York
**Titles**

*Geronimo* (2006)

*The Girl Who Married the Moon: Tales from Native North America* (2006)

*Hidden Roots* (2006)

*Jim Thorpe, Original All-American* (2006)

*The Return of Skeleton Man* (2006)

*The Arrow over the Door* (1998)

*The Earth Under Sky Bear's Feet: Native American Poems of the Land* (1998)

*Flying With the Eagle, Racing the Great Bear: Stories from Native North America* (1998)

*The Heart of a Chief* (1998)

*When the Chenoo Howls* (1998)

*Eagle Song* (1997)

*Tell Me a Tale* (1997)

*Keepers of Life* (1997)

*Children of the Longhouse* (1996)

*Dog People: Native American Stories* (1995)

*First Strawberries: A Cherokee Story* (1993)

*Thirteen Moons on a Turtle's Back: A Native American Year of Moons* (1992)

*Keepers of the Animals* (1991)

**Interesting Information**

- Raised by his grandparents, Bruchac is an avid reader from childhood and lives in the same house in which he was raised.

- Bruchac plays guitar, flute, and drum—sometimes he plays songs he writes.

- Bruchac says we must learn to listen to each other and to the earth.

- He won the Virginia Hamilton Literary Award for his efforts in preserving Native traditions, issues, and concerns that are important to contemporary Native cultures.

**Web Site:** http://www.josephbruchac.com

**Contact:**
P.O. Box 308
Greenfield Center, NY 12833
Phone: (518) 584-1728
Fax: (518) 583-9741
E-mail: nudatlog@earthlink.net

# Annotated Journal Article

Starnes, Bobby Ann. "What We Don't Know Can Hurt Them: White Teachers, Indian Children." *Phi Delta Kappan* (January 1, 2006): 384.

    White teachers who may have many years of experience find themselves unprepared when they teach Indian Children: "they don't understand the history, the communities, and learning need of their children." The author includes practices for best learning, emphasis on the resiliency of Native Americans, discussion of Native American in history textbooks to tell the white man's story, and cultural fables in the discovery of America and our Thanksgiving tradition. White teachers should be encouraged to find a mentor in the Indian community, get educated about tribal history, know and participate in the community, question personal knowledge of historical facts, create appropriate materials, expect measured success, and strive for more training.

# Resources

## Books

Benes, Rebecca C. *Native American Picturebooks of Change: The Art of Historic Children's Editions.* Museum of New Mexico Press, 2004. ISBN 0-89013-471-5

Keoke, Emory Dean, and Kay Marie Porterfield. *Encyclopedia of American Indian Contributions to the World.* Facts on File, 2002. ISBN 0-8160-4052-4

Molin Paulette Fairbanks. *American Indian Themes in Young Adult Literature.* Scarecrow Press, 2005. ISBN 0-8108-5081-8

*Native Americans.* 10 vols. Grolier, 2000. ISBN 0-7172-9395-5

*Student Almanac of Native American History.* 2 vols. Greenwood, 2003. ISBN 0-313-32599-5 Middle School

*UXL Encyclopedia of Native American Tribes.* 4 vols. UXL, 1999. ISBN 0-7876-2838-7 Middle School

Waldman, Carl. *Encyclopedia of Native American Tribes.* Facts on File, 2006. ISBN 0-8160-6273-0

_____. *Atlas of the North American Indian.* Facts on File, 2000. ISBN 0-8160-3974-7

York, Sherry. *Children's and Young Adult Literature by Native Americans: A Concept Guide for Librarians, Teachers, Parents, and Students.* Linworth, Inc., 2003. ISBN 1-58683-119-4

## Organizations

American Indian Science and Engineering Society
2305 Revard SE, Suite 200
Albuquerque, NM 87106
http://www.aises.org

Bureau of Indian Affairs
1849 C Street NW
Washington, DC 20245
(202) 208-3711

Council for Indian Education
1240 Burlington Ave.
Billings, MT 59102-4224
(406) 248-3465
http://www.cie-mt.org

Cradleboard Teaching Project
1191 Kuhio Highway,
Kapaa, HI 96746
(808) 822-3111
http://www.cradleboard.org

Oyate (Native organization that evaluates materials about Native Americans)
2702 Mathews Street
Berkeley, Ca 94702
(510) 848-6700
http://www.oyate.org

## Web Sites

**Alaska Native Heritage Center:** http://www.alaskanative.net

*Canku Ota (Many Paths): A Newsletter Celebrating Native America:* http://www.turtletrack.org

**Cynthia Leitich Smith Children's Literature Resources:** http://www.cynthialeitichsmith.com/index1.htm

**Hanksville (homepages of native authors):** http://www.hanksville.org

*Indian Country Today* (weekly newspaper covering national issues): http://www.Indiancountry.com

**National Museum of the American Indian:** http://www.nmai.si.edu

**Native American Sites:** http://www.nativeculture.com/lisamitten/indians.html

**Native Nations (official and unofficial tribal sites):** http://www.kstrom.net/isk/tribes/tribes/htm

**Native Peoples: Arts & Lifeways:** http://www.nativepeoples.com

**Native Web** (culture from the Arctic to Tierra del Fuego): http://www.nativeweb.org

*News from Indian Country* **(published twice a month):** http://www.indiancountrynews.com

**Smithsonian's National Museum of the American Indian:** http://www.AmericanIndian.si.edu

# Awards

## American Indian Youth Literature Award (New 2006)

The American Indian Library Association (AILA), an affiliate of the American Library Association (ALA), created this award to identify and honor the very best writing and illustrations by and about Native American Indians.

### Picture Book

Confederated Salish and Kootenai Tribes. *Beaver Steals Fire: A Salish Coyote Story*.

### Middle School

Erdrich, Louise. *The Birchbark House*.

### Young Adult

Bruchac, Joseph. *Hidden Roots*.

# Chapter *10*

# White/European

## Introduction

"Anyone who could buy a ticket" to America or walk across its borders was called an immigrant during the late eighteenth century. From 1820 to 1870, the new immigrants were from northern and western Europe, 1.7 million Irish immigrants arrived between 1841 and 1860 as a result of the potato famine. At this same time, about the same number of Germans settled in America. Today, the days of unlimited immigration are over. Beginning with 1978, no more than 20,000 people may emigrate annually from any one country. During 1981–1990, 761,500 immigrants were from Europe. This number is small compared with immigrant numbers from Asia and Latin America.

## Definition

**White:** A person having origins in any of the original peoples of Europe, the Middle East, or North Africa. It includes people who indicate their race as "White" or as Irish, German, Italian, Lebanese, Near Easterner, Arab, or Polish. (Magazine Publishers of America)

# Annotations

Bartoletti, Susan Campbell. *Dreaming of America: An Ellis Island Story.* Troll, 2000. ISBN 0-8167-6520-0 Gr. 2–4

Annie Moore, age fourteen, left Ireland aboard the S.S. *Nevada* with her two younger brothers to reunite with her parents who had left Ireland three years previously. They cross the ocean and arrive in New York Harbor on Annie's birthday. Annie makes history by being the first immigrant to enter America through Ellis Island. She is given a ten-dollar gold piece to commemorate the event. "A statue of Annie and her brothers stands of the quay at Cobh, Ireland, where their journey began. Another stands on Ellis Island, where their journey ended.

_____. *Growing Up in Coal Country.* Houghton Mifflin, 1996. ISBN 0-395-77847-6 Gr. 4–7

Oral history and archival documents are used to piece together the story of children's lives in the coal country of northeastern Pennsylvania during the nineteenth and twentieth centuries. Many of the children were immigrants, and the boys, even though they might have been younger, were passed off as fourteen years old and put to work. Black-and-white photos and the narrative tell the story.

Bunting, Eve. *A Picnic in October.* Harcourt Brace, 1999. ISBN 0-15-201656-2 Gr. K–3

Every year Tony and his family meet his grandparents, cousins, and extended family, and they take the ferry to the Statue of Liberty. They spread a blanket on the grass and have a picnic under the watchful eyes of Lady Liberty. Tony at first is embarrassed when they light the birthday candles and Grandma blows them out. Especially when they all blow kisses to Lady Liberty as grandma gives thanks for taking her in. But when Tony sees some new Americans standing in solemn reverence, he gets a sense of his grandmother's feelings.

Couric, Katie. *The Brand New Kid.* Doubleday, 2000. ISBN 0-385-50030-0 Gr. K–2

Lazlo S. Gasky is the new kid in school and town, and he does not fit in with the rest of the children. They taunt and tease him, and he keeps his head down until Ellie decides to see if she can change how the kids are treating him. She asks if he would like to play and then spends the afternoon at his house. Lazlo is different because he has an accent, but Ellie knows that if the other kids give him a chance, they will like him.

Gundisch, Karin. *How I Became an American.* Cricket Books, 2001. ISBN 0-8126-4875-7 Gr. 3–7

This winner of the Batchelder Award follows the journey of a family emigrating from Germany to America during the early 1900s. Mama asks Johann to write everything down so that they will never forget. Johann's father and eldest brother leave for Youngstown, Ohio, first and later send for the rest of the family. The journey is long and hard, and life in Youngstown is not easy. The children of the family are able to adapt to the new lifestyle easier than the parents. Johann "relays the many differences between the two lifestyles and cultures."

Lombard, Jenny. *Drita: My Homegirl.* G. P. Putnam's Sons, 2006. ISBN 0-399-24380-1 Gr. 3–5

Drita, together with her mother, grandmother, and younger brother, join her father, whom they haven't seen in over a year. Ten-year-old Drita does not speak English and is an immigrant from Kosovo. At school, Drita becomes more interested in Maxine after Maxie stands up for Drita when a fellow student is bullying her. As their friendship develops, they two girls visit each other's homes and help each other with their troubles. They are quite a pair, Maxie and her homegirl, Drita.

# Bibliography

Aksomitis, Linda. *Adeline's Dream.* Coteau Books, 2006. ISBN 1-55050-323-5 Gr. 4–7

Blume, Judy. *Starring Sally J. Freedman as Herself.* Dell Yearling, 1986. ISBN 0-440-48253-4 Gr. 3–7

Frost, Helen. *The Braid.* Farrar, Straus & Giroux, 2006. ISBN 0-374-30962-0 Young Adult

Glaser, Linda. *Bridge to America: Based on a True Story.* Houghton Mifflin, 2005. ISBN 0-618-56301-6 Gr. 4–6

Mead, Alice. *Swimming to America.* Farrar, Straus & Giroux, 2005. ISBN 0-374-38047-3 Gr. 7–12

Nolan, Han. *A Summer of Kings.* Harcourt Children's Books, 2006. ISBN 0-15-205108-2 Young Adult

Pastore, Clare. *Fiona's McGilray's Story: A Voyage from Ireland in 1849.* Penguin Group, 2001. ISBN 0-425-17783-1 Gr. 4–7

Raphael, Marie. *Streets of Gold: A Novel.* Source Productions, 1998. ISBN 1-883088-05-4 Gr. 6–9

Snell, Gordon, ed. *Thicker than Water: Coming of Age Stories by Irish and Irish-American Writers.* Turtleback Books, 2001. ISBN 0-606-22182-4 General Adult

Stone, B. J. *Ola's Wake.* Sagebrush Education Resources, 2002. ISBN 0-613-55345-4 Gr. 3-6

## Picture Books

Aliki. *Painted Words/Spoken Memories: Marianthe's Story.* Greenwillow, 1998. ISBN 0-688-15661-4 Gr. K–3

Atwell, Debby. *The Thanksgiving Door.* Houghton Mifflin, 2006. ISBN 0-618-77124-7 Gr. PS–3

Bunting, Eve. *Picnic in October.* Harcourt Children's Books, 2004. ISBN 0-15-205065-5 Gr. K–3

Buzzeo, Toni. *The Sea Chest.* Dial, 2002. ISBN 0-8037-2703-8 Gr. 0 & up

Cohen, Barbara. *Molly's Pilgrim.* HarperCollins, 1998. ISBN 0-688-16279-7 Gr. PS–3

DiSalvo-Ryan, DyAnne. *Grandpa's Corner Store.* HarperCollins, 2000. ISBN 0-688-16716-0 Gr. 0–3

Winter, Jeanette. *Klara's New World.* Random House, 1992. ISBN 0-679-90626-1 Gr. K–1

Woodruff, Elvira. *Small Beauties: The Journey of Darcy Heart O'Hara.* Knopf, 2006. ISBN 0-375-82686-6 Gr. 1–4

## Nonfiction

Freedman, Russell. *Immigrant Kids.* Scholastic, 1980. ISBN 0-525-32538-7 Gr. 2–6

Hoobler, Dorothy. *Scholastic History of Immigration.* Scholastic Reference, 2003. ISBN 0-439-16297-1 Gr. 5–9

Maestro, Betsy. *Coming to America: The Story of Immigration.* Scholastic, 1996. ISBN 0-590-44151-5 Gr. K–4

Morrow, Robert. *Immigration: Blessing or Burden.* Lerner, 1997. ISBN 0-8225-2613-1 Gr. 6–10

Murphy, Jim. *Pick and Shovel Poet: The Journeys of Pascal D'Angelo.* Clarion, 2000. ISBN 0-395-77610-4 Gr. 6 & up

## Series

*Immigrants in America.* Chelsea House

# Discussion Questions

- Is immigration a good thing or a bad thing for our country?

- Do you think it is more difficult or easier for people from Europe to immigrate to the United States now?

- Do you think we should strengthen our borders to prevent migration from the south and north?

- Do you think that new immigrants work hard and fill jobs that many Americans do not want to do?

- It is easier for those of white/European heritage to become part of the American culture?

- Do Italian, Polish, and Irish communities still exist in major cities?

- Why is it difficult for older immigrants to become part of the American culture?

# Featured Author

## Eve Bunting

**Birthplace:** Maghera, Northern Ireland
**Date of Birth:** December 19, 1928
**Current Home:** Pasadena, CA
**Titles**

*Anna's Table* (2003)

*The Presence: A Ghost Story* (2003)

*Seriously Stinky Trainers* (2003)

*Whales Passing* (2003)

*The Bones of Fred McFee* (2002)

*Girls: A to Z* (2002)

*Little Badger's Just-About Birthday* (2002)

*One Candle* (2002)

*The Days of Summer* (2001)

*Gleam and Glow* (2001)

*Jin Woo* (2001)

*Little Badger, Terror of the Seven Seas* (2001)

*Peepers* (2001)

*Riding the Tiger* (2001)

*The Summer of Riley* (2001)

*Too Many Monsters* (2001)

*Can You Do This, Old Badger?* (2000)

*Dear Wish Fairy* (2000)

*Doll Baby* (2000)

*Dreaming of America: An Ellis Island Story* (2000)

*I Like the Way You Are* (2000)

*The Memory String* (2000)

*Swan in Love* (2000)

*Wanna Buy an Alien?* (2000)

*Who Was Born This Special Day?* (2000)

*Blackwater* (1999)

*Butterfly House* (1999)

*I Have an Olive Tree* (1999)

*A Picnic in October* (1999)

*Rudi's Pond* (1999)

*The Day the Whale Came* (1998)

*So Far from the Sea* (1998)

*December* (1997)

*Ducky* (1997)

*I Am the Mummy Heb-Nefert* (1997)

*Moonstick: The Seasons of the Sioux* (1997)

*My Backpack* (1997)

*On Call Back Mountain* (1997)

*The Pumpkin Fair* (1997)

*Some Frog!* (1997)

*Trouble on the T-ball Team* (1997)

*Twinnies* (1997)

*Your Move* (1997)

**Interesting Information**

- Bunting is the author of more than one hundred books for young readers (picture books, novels, and nonfiction).

- In 1958, she emigrated to the United States, where she has lived ever since, raising three children and—more recently—welcoming four grandchildren.

- Bunting began writing after moving to California, where she enrolled in a community college creative writing course.

**Web Site:** http://books.scholastic.com/teachers/authorsandbooks/authorstudies/authorhome.jsp?authorID=202&displayName=Biography

**Contact:**
Eve Bunting
c/o Clarion Books
215 Park Avenue South
New York, NY 100030

# Annotated Journal Article

Lamme, Linda, Danling Fu, and Ruth Lowery. "Immigrants as Portrayed in Children's Picture Books." *The Social Studies* (May/June, 2004): 123–28.

Picture books about immigrant children and their lives in America help others understand the challenges and help validate the lives of immigrant children. According to the article, there are three parts: the transition, the connection, and becoming American. It is important that the titles accurately describe these three steps, and the fact is, many do not. Not all diversity stories have happy endings; many describe the harsh realities of everyday life.

# Resources

## Books

Hitchcock, Jeff. *Lifting the White Veil: An Exploration of White American Culture in a Multiracial Context.* Crandall Dostie & Douglass Books, 2003. ISBN 0-971-90171-8

## Organizations

INS Experts
12280 Saratoga Sunnyvale Road—Suite 116
Saratoga, CA 95070

Federation for American Immigration Reform
1666 Connecticut Avenue NW, Suite 400
Washington, DC 20009

## Web Sites

**American Family Immigration History Center:** http://www.ellisisland.org

**CensusScope:** Census 2000 data, charts, maps and rankings: http://www.censusscope.org/index

**Ellis Island:** http://www.history.com/minisites/ellisisland

**Federation for American Immigration Reform:** http://www.fairus.org/history

**From One Life to Another:** http://library.thinkquest.org/26786/en/introduction/help.php3

**Immigration History Research Center:** http://www.ihrc.umn.edu

**The New Americans:** http://www.pbs.org/independentlens/newamericans

**Scholastic.com Teachers—Immigration:** http://teacher.scholastic.com/activities/immigration/index

**U.S. Citizen and Immigration Services:** http://www.insexperts.com

**Welcome to the United States: A Guide for New Immigrants:** http://www.uscis.gov/graphics/citizenship/imm_guide.htm

# Awards

## Carter G. Woodson Book Award Winners

National Council for the Social Studies established the Carter G. Woodson Book Awards in 1974, for the most distinguished social science books appropriate for young readers that depict ethnicity in the United States.

### *2006 Award Winners*

**Elementary Level Award Winner**
Raven, Margot Theis. *Let Them Play.* 2005.

**Elementary Level Honor Book**
Winter, Johan. *Roberto Clemente: Pride of the Pittsburgh.* 2005.

**Middle-Level Award Winner**
Cruz, Barbara. *César Chávez: A Voice for Farmworkers.* 2005.

**Middle-Level Honor Book**
Marquez, Heron. *Roberto Clemente: Baseball's Humanitarian Hero.* 2004.

**Secondary-Level Award Winner**
Miller, Calvin Craig. *No Easy Answers: Baynard Rustin and the Civil Rights Movement.* 2005

**Secondary Level Honor Book**
Duggleby, John. *Uh Huh! The Story of Ray Charles.* 2005

# Chapter *11*

# Ageism

## Introduction

In years gone by, older people were simply that—they passed the time quietly, often in poor health, cared for by younger generations of relatives, often not even able to care for the younger children in the family. How times have changes! Aging Americans are more active than ever before. They retire later, go back to school, travel, are in better health, are more financially stable, log in countless hours volunteering, serve as mentors, and enjoy life! Who would have ever thought that John Glenn, Jr. would have been an astronaut on a nine-day mission on the space shuttle at age seventy-seven!

## Definition

**Ageism:** Referring to a person's age in a context in which age is not relevant reinforces U.S. society's emphasis on youth as the optimum stage of life. In the workforce, "older workers" become another group to be demeaned or protected. In the media, women are often designated as "grandmothers" when their maternal and grand-maternal status is irrelevant. (Magazine Publishers of America)

# Annotations

Bauer, Joan. *Rules of the Road.* G.P. Putnam's Sons, 1998. ISBN 0-399-23140-4 Gr. 7–12

Jenna works at a shoe store for the summer, and her ways catch the attention of the elderly owner. She becomes the owner's driver, and they go on a six-week trip to visit company shoe stores and keep the woman's young son from forcing her out of the business.

Brooks, Martha. *Being with Henry.* Douglas & McIntyre, Limited, 1999. ISBN 0-88899-377-3 Juvenile

Sixteen-year-old Laker was thrown out of his house after a fight with his stepfather. He spends three weeks on his own. Two days in a row, an older man, Henry, hands him nickels and quarters. On the second day, Henry returns and asks if he does yard work. Laker moves in with Henry and helps around the house, attends school, and pays rent. Laker is company for Henry, whose wife recently died. Gradually Laker begins to trust Henry and his granddaughter, Charlene.

Cooney, Caroline B. *Hit the Road.* Dell, 2006. ISBN 0-385-90174-7 Young Adult

Sixteen-year-old Brittany, with a new driver's license and her parents away on a trip, becomes an illegal chauffeur of a rental car. Her eighty-six-year old grandmother has rented the car to pick up three former classmates to go on a fairly long road trip to their college reunion. Nannie is unable to drive the car, so Brittany does, and the trip is filled with wild driving, forgotten directions, an unscrupulous son, theft, a kidnapping, and a clear understanding of what it is like to be in your eighties and having others make decisions for you.

Fox, Mem. *Wilfrid Gordon McDonald Partridge.* Kane Miller, 1989. ISBN 0-916291-26-X Gr. PS–3

Wilfred lives next door to a nursing home and often visits the residents. His favorite is Miss Nancy because she has four names, like he does. He overhears his parents talking about Miss Nancy, and they say she has lost her memory. Wilfred asks everyone what a memory is. Everyone has a different definition. But in the end, his efforts help Miss Nancy to remember many things!

Giff, Patricia Reilly. *Pictures of Hollis Woods.* Random House, 2002. ISBN 0-385-90070-8 Gr. 4–8

Hollis was abandoned at birth and has lived in many foster homes. She decides she likes Josie, a retired art teacher, her most recent foster mom. Twelve-year-old Hollis is artistically talented and bonds with Josie as they enjoy creating art together. She sees that Josie is becoming more and more forgetful, and she worries about what will happen to her. She also misses her favorite foster family, the Regans. As Josie's dementia gets worse, Hollis stays home with her, and then eventually they runaway to the Regans because Hollis is afraid that if the social worker finds out, she will move Hollis to another foster home.

Kimmel, Elizabeth Cody. *Visiting Miss Caples.* Sagebrush Education Resources, 2001. ISBN 0-613-44428-0 Gr. 5–8

The service project for the year is to visit with an elderly person weekly. When Jen went to visit with Miss Caples, she could not get a reaction of any sort for the whole hour. At first, Jen would read to her, then she began to talk to her about her problems at school and with her best friend, Liv. Jen adored her lively, beautiful, and popular friend, but she is noticing that Liv can be very cruel to those who cross her. After many visits, Miss Caples finally begins to talk to Jen and tells her about a similar relationship she had with her best friend when she was at a boarding school. Miss Caples warns Jen that Liv may be dangerous and gives Jen the impetus and strength to break off their friendship.

Yolen, Jane. *Miz Berlin Walks.* Penguin Group, 2000. ISBN 0-698-11845-6 Gr. PS–3

A little black girl tells the story of her neighbor, Miz Berlin, a very elderly white lady who would walk a full block each night. The girl, Mary Louise, eventually walked a short distance wither each night, just to listen to her stories. They did this for a long, long time until one day Miz Berlin did not come, and Mary Louise found out that she had fallen and broken her hip. She never walked the street again; bedridden and feeble at home, she eventually died. But then Mary Louise would imagine her each evening walking down the street and remember her wonderful stories.

# Bibliography

Adler, C. S. *One Unhappy Horse.* Houghton Mifflin, 2001. ISBN 0-618-04912-6 Gr. 4–6

Almond, David. *Kit's Wilderness.* Doubleday, 2000. ISBN 0-385-32665-3 Gr. 7 & up

Auch, Mary Jane. *Wing Nut.* Henry Holt, 2005. ISBN 0-8050-7531-3 Gr. 3–6

Bauer, Joan. *Best Foot Forward.* Penguin Group, 2005. ISBN 0-399-23474-3 Young Adult

Bogart, JoEllen. *Jeremiah Learns to Read.* Scholastic, 1999. ISBN 0-531-30190-7 Gr. 0–4

Caletti, Deb. *Honey, Baby, Sweetheart.* Simon & Schuster, 2004. ISBN 0-689-86765-4 Young Adult

Cheng, Andrea. *Grandfather Counts.* Lee & Low, 2000. ISBN 1-58430-010-8 Gr. K–4

Flood, Pansie Hart. *Sylvia and Miz Lula Maye.* Carolrhoda, 2003. ISBN 0-87614-204-8 Gr. 3–6

Glick, Susan. *One Shot.* Henry Holt, 2003. ISBN 0-8050-6844-9 Young Adult

Greene, Stephanie. *Falling into Place.* Houghton Mifflin, 2002. ISBN 0-618-17744-2 Gr. 4–6

_____. *Queen Sophie Hartley.* Houghton Mifflin, 2005. ISBN 0-618-49461-8 Gr. 3–5

Holt, Kimberly Willis. *Dancing in Cadillac Light.* Penguin Group, 2001. ISBN 0-698-111970-3 Gr. 5 & up

Kvasnosky, Laura McGee. *Zelda and Ivy One Christmas.* Candlewick Press, 2002. ISBN 0-7636-1344-4 Gr. 0–4

Laminack, Lester L. *The Sunsets of Miss Olivia Wiggins.* Peachtree, 1998. ISBN 1-56145-139-8 Gr. 1–5

Mills, Claudia, *Makeovers by Marcia.* Farrar, Straus & Giroux, 2005. ISBN 0-374-34654-2 Juvenile

Nixon, Joan Lowery. *Nobody's There.* Sagebrush Education Resources, 2001. ISBN 0-613-36851-7 Gr. 7–12

Rylant, Cynthia. *Henry and Mudge and the Great Grandpas.* Simon & Schuster, 2005. ISBN 0-689-81170-5 Gr. 0–3

_____. *The Old Woman Who Names Things.* Book Wholesalers, Inc., 2002. ISBN 0-7587-3314-6 Juvenile

Siebold, Jan. *Doing Time Online.* Albert Whitman, 2002. ISBN 0-8075-5959-8 Gr. 4–7

Tremblay, Carole. *The Old Man and the C.* Pineapple Press, 2006. ISBN 1-56164-354-8 Gr. 2–5

## Picture Books

Briggs, Raymond. *Jim and the Beanstalk.* Penguin Group, 1997. ISBN 0-698-11577-5 Gr. PS–3

Bunting, Eve. *Sunshine Home.* Clarion, 1994. ISBN 0-395-63309-5 Gr. 0–3

_____. *The Wednesday Surprise.* Houghton Mifflin, 1989. ISBN 0-395-54776-8 Gr. 0–3

Capdevila, Roser. *Grandparents!* Kane Miller, 2003. ISBN 1-929132-46-8 Juvenile

Carlson, Nancy. *Hooray for Grandparents Day!* Penguin, 2002. ISBN 0-14-230125-6 Juvenile

Hest, Amy. *Mr. George Baker.* Candlewick Press, 2004. ISBN 0-7636-1233-7 Gr. 0–3

Leedahl, Shelley A. *The Bone Talker.* Red Deer Press, 2004. ISBN 0-88995-214-0 Gr. PS–3

Proimos, James. *Joe's Wish.* Harcourt, 1998. ISBN 0-15-201831-X Gr. PS–3

Shriver, Maria. *What's Happening to Grandpa?* Little, Brown and Company, 2004. ISBN 0-316-00101-5 Gr. 1–4

Spalding, Andrea. *Me and Mr. Mah.* Orca Book Publishers, 2000. ISBN 1-55143-168-8 Gr. PS–3

Uslander, Arlene. *That's What Grandparents Are For.* Peel Productions, 2001. ISBN 0-939217-60-0 Gr. PS–3

Winch, John. *The Old Woman Who Loved to Read.* Holiday House, 1997. ISBN 0-8234-1281-4 Gr. PS–3

## Nonfiction

Helmer, Diana Star. *Let's Talk About When Someone You Love Is in a Nursing Home.* Rosen, 1999. ISBN 0-82389-5190-1 Gr. 3 & up

Lakin, Patricia. *Grandparents: Around the World.* Thomson Gale, 1999. ISBN 1-56711-146-7 Gr. 3–6

Wilkinson, Beth. *Coping When a Grandparent Has Alzheimer's Disease.* Rosen, 1995. ISBN 0-8239-1947-1 Gr. 7–12

# Discussion Questions

- What effect are baby boomers having on retirement numbers?
- How active are boomers as grandparents?
- Do you appreciate the age and experiences of your grandparents?
- Are older people making more contributions than before?
- What age is "old"?
- Are older people respected?

# Featured Author

## Mem Fox

**Birthplace:** Melbourne, Australia
**Date of Birth:** March 1946
**Current Home:** Adelaide, Australia
**Titles**

*Hunwick's Egg* (2005)

*Where Is The Green Sheep?* (2004)

*The Magic Hat* (2002)

*Harriet, You'll Drive Me Wild!* (2000)

*Sleepy Bears* (1999)

*Whoever You Are* (1998)

*Boo to a Goose* (1996)

*Wombat Divine* (1995)

*Tough Boris* (1994)

*Time for Bed* (1993)

*Memories* (1992)

*Shoes from Grandpa* (1989)

*Night Noises* (1989)

*Guess What?* (1988)

*Koala Lou* (1988)

*Arabella, the Smallest Girl in the World* (1986)

*Hattie and the Fox* (1986)

*Wilfrid Gordon McDonald Partridge* (1984)

*Possum Magic* (1983)

**Interesting Information**

- *Possum Magic* is the best-selling children's book ever in Australia, with sales of more than 2 million.

- *Time for Bed* is on Oprah's list of the twenty best children's books of all time.

- Fox was an associate professor in Literacy Studies at Flinders University in Adelaide, Australia, where she taught teachers for twenty-four years.

**Web Site:** http://www.memfox.com/welcome.html

**Contact:** Mem Fox has a guestbook on her Web site: http://www.memfox.net/guestbook/

# Annotated Journal Articles

Gattilia, Lauren. "Books Celebrate Grandparent-Grandchild Bond." *Education World* (September, 2000). Available at http://www.education-world.com/a_books/books160.shtml
    When President Jimmy Carter declared a National Grandparents Day in 1978, the bond between grandparents and grandchildren was celebrated. This article reviews four titles about this special relationship.

University of Florida. "UF Study: Grandparents celebrated instead of reviled in children's lit." *Science Blog* (December 2001). Available at: http://www.scienceblog.com
    A University of Florida study of sixty-four randomly selected titles from Books in Print published after 1985 showed that all but three titles represented grandparents as upbeat, independent, and wise. The study concluded that grandparents are getting more attention because of medical advances and because they are living longer and healthier lives. More than half of the authors of the titles dedicated their stories to their grandparents or grandchildren.

# Resources

## Books

Linsley, Leslie. *Totally Cool Grandparenting: A Practical Handbook of Tips, Hints, & Activities for the Modern Grandparent.* St. Martin's Press, 1997. ISBN 0-312-17047-5

Richmond, Marianne. *The Gifts of Being Grand: For Grandparents Everywhere.* Marianne Richmond Studios, 2003. ISBN 0-9652448-8-1

Truly, Traci. *Grandparents' Rights.* Sphinx, 2005. ISBN 1-57248-526-4

Weil, Andrew. *Healthy Aging: A Lifelong Guide to Your Physical and Spiritual Well-Being.* Knopf, 2005. ISBN 0-375-40755-3

## Organizations

American Association for Retired People
601 E Street NW
Washington, DC 20049

National Council on Aging
300 D Street, SW Suite 801
Washington, D.C. 20024

The SPRY Foundation
3916 Rosemary Street
Chevy Chase, MD 20815

## Web Sites

**American Association for Retired People:** http://www.aarp.org/

**National Council on Aging:** http://www.ncoa.org/

**Service Corps of Retired Executives:** http://www.score.org/

**Setting Priorities for Retirement Years:** http://www.spry.org/

**The Seniors Coalition:** http://www.senior.org/

**Generations United:** http://www.gu.orga

# Chapter 12

# Exceptionalities

## Introduction

Children and young adults with both physical and mental exceptionalities still have difficulty in our society. They still get called names and are excluded from circles of friends and activities. In 1975, the Education for All Handicapped Children Act required a free and appropriate education with related services for each child in the least restrictive environment. This created inclusion, the practice of educating all or most children with physical, mental, and developmental disabilities in regular classrooms. Often, a special assistant to the classroom teacher was required. Therefore, students with exceptionalities were mixed in with regular kids, and students were exposed to greater diversity than ever before. Unfortunately, this did not make it easier for those with exceptionalities, nor did it seem to keep the regular kids from teasing.

## Definition

**Exceptionalities:** Deviating widely from a norm, as of physical or mental ability. (http://www.dictionary.com)

# Annotations

Bennett, James W. *Blue Star Rapture.* Turtleback Books, 2001. ISBN 0-606-20574-8 Gr. 9 & up
T.J. pretended to help Tyrone, and in doing so he felt important. Coaches knew that T.J. looked out for the big guy, Tyrone, and asked him to encourage Tyrone and keep track of any of his communications with other scouts for colleges. After the two of them go to Full Court, a basketball camp, T.J. realizes that he is a work in transition. In the future, he is out of the loop with Tyrone. T.J is a good player in his own way and needs to perfect himself. The book contains mature language.

Koertge, Ronald. *Stoner & Spaz.* Candlewick Press, 2002. ISBN 0-7636-1608-7 Gr. 8–12
Sixteen-year-old Ben Bancroft has cerebral palsy and lives with his grandmother. He is a loner who is addicted to old movies. Colleen Minou is always high, her clothes are from the Salvation Army, she is tattooed everywhere, and she has a foul mouth. They become a couple. She is the first one who ever really notices Ben and who actually has the nerve to tease him about his disability. She takes him to clubs, gives him his first joint, and actually challenges him to direct his own movie. He challenges her to get off the drugs—but she is unable to do so—what will happen to Ben, who is seriously addicted to Colleen?

Park, Barbara. *The Graduation of Jake Moon.* Simon & Schuster, 2002. ISBN 0-689-839855 Gr. 4–6
Jake and two eighth-grade friends are on the way home from school when they begin to make fun of an old man in a dumpster. Jake lets it happen and doesn't let on that the old man is his grandfather, Skelly. Jake was always very close with his grandfather, but he doesn't know how to handle Skelly's Alzheimer's disease. As Jake reminisces about Skelly, his guilt lessens, and he reconciles with Skelly. Jake is forced to publicly acknowledge and rescue his grandfather during his eighth-grade graduation.

Sones, Sonya. *Stop Pretending: What Happened When My Big Sister Went Crazy.* HarperCollins, 1999. ISBN 0-06-446218-8 Gr. 3–7
An intimate story of what it was like for the author when her elder sister was hospitalized for a mental breakdown. This story is told through successive poems that express sorrow, bewilderment, loss, fear, loneliness, and happiness. The author shares her understanding of mental illness and its consequences on the family. In the author's note at the end of the short book, she states that the sister is now married and takes medicine to keep her disease under control.

Trueman, Terry. *Stuck in Neutral.* HarperCollins, 2001. ISBN 0-06-447213-2 Gr. 5 & up
Shawn McDaniel is a teenager with profound cerebral palsy who is unable to communicate at all with those around him. He is intelligent, he can read, and has an amazing memory, but he cannot share any of this with his family. His father has begun research for a biography of a man who smothers his profoundly disabled child. So Shawn is convinced that his father is going to kill him because his father thinks Shawn's life is an endless torment and that he suffers with no reason and no hope. Shawn has no way to tell his father how rich his life really is.

# Bibliography

Christopher, Matt. *Wheel Wizards.* Little, Brown and Company, 2000. ISBN 0-316-13611-5 Gr. 3–7 Wheelchair Confinement

Coleman, Michael. *On the Run.* Penguin, 2004. ISBN 0-525-47318-1 Young Adult Blind

Day, Alexandra. *The Flight of a Dove.* Farrar, Straus & Giroux, 2004. ISBN 0-374-39952-2 Gr. 3–5 Autism

Deans, Sis Boulos. *Rainy.* Henry Holt, 2005. ISBN 0-8050-7831-2 Gr. 3–7 Attention-Deficit/Hyperactivity Disorder

Dodds, Bill. *My Sister Annie.* Boyds Mills, 2003. ISBN 1-56397-554-8 Gr. 4–6 Down Syndrome

Dorris, Michael. *Sees Behind Trees.* Sagebrush Education Resources, 1997. ISBN 0-613-05850-X Gr. 3–6 Vision Problems

Draper, Sharon. *Double Dutch.* Simon & Schuster, 2003. ISBN 0-689-84231-7 Juvenile Learning Disability

Evangelista, Beth. *Gifted.* Walker & Company, 2005. ISBN 0-8027-8994-3 Gr. 5–9 Gifted

Farrell, Mame. *Marrying Malcolm Murgatroyd.* Farrar, Straus & Giroux, 1998. ISBN 0-374-44744-6 Gr. 4–7 Muscular Dystrophy

Ferris, Jean. *Of Sound Mind.* Farrar, Straus & Giroux, 2004. ISBN 0-374-45584-8 Young Adult Deaf

Hamilton, Virginia. *Bluish.* Scholastic, 1999. ISBN 0-590-28879-2 Gr. 4–9 Leukemia

Heisel, Sharon. *Eyes of a Stranger.* Doubleday, 1996. ISBN 0-385-31727-1 General Adult (for mature readers) Physical Disability

Kehret, Pat. *Earthquake Terror.* Penguin Group, 1998. ISBN 0-14-038343-3 Gr. 3–7 Physical Disability

_____. *My Brother Made Me Do It.* Simon & Schuster, 2001. ISBN 0-671-03419-7 Juvenile Pediatric Rheumatoid Arthritis

Kinsey-Warnock, Natalie. *Lumber Camp Library.* HarperCollins, 2003. ISBN 0-06-444292-6 Gr. 2–5 Learning Disability

Konigsburg, E.L. *The View from Saturday.* Simon & Schuster, 1998. ISBN 0-689-81721-5 Gr. 3–7 Wheelchair Confinement

Lord, Cynthia. *Rules.* Scholastic, 2006. ISBN 0-439-44382-2 Gr. 4–7 Autism

Martin, Ann. *A Corner of the Universe.* Scholastic, 2002. ISBN 0-439-38880-5 Gr. 5–8 Mental Retardation

Matlin, Marlee. *Deaf Child Crossing.* Simon & Schuster, 2002. ISBN 0-689-82208-1 Gr. 3–6 Deaf

McElfresh, Lynn E. *Can You Feel the Thunder?* Simon & Schuster, 1999. ISBN 0-689-82324-X Gr. 4–8 Blind and Deaf

McNamee, Graham. *Sparks.* Random House, 2002. ISBN 0-385-72977-4 Gr. 2–5 Learning Disabilities

Mikaelson, Ben. *Petey.* Disney Press, 1998. ISBN 0-7868-0426-2 Gr. 5 & up Cerebral Palsy

Mitchell, Marianne. *Finding Zola.* Boyds Mills, 2003. ISBN 1-59078-070-1 Young Adult Wheelchair Confinement

Nolan, Han. *A Face in Every Window.* Penguin Group, 2001. ISBN 0-14-131218-1 Young Adult Mental Retardation

Philbrick, Rodman. *Freak the Mighty.* Turtleback Books, 1993. ISBN 0-606-07540-2 Juvenile Birth Defects

Robb, Diane. *The Alphabet Wars: A Story About Dyslexia.* Albert Whitman, 2004. ISBN 0-8075-0302-9 Gr. 2–5 Dyslexia

Rottman, S. L. *Head above Water.* Peachtree, 2003. ISBN 1-56145-238-6 Young Adult Down Syndrome

Scrimger, Richard. *From Charlie's Point of View.* Dutton's Children's Books, 2005. ISBN 0525473742 Gr. 5–8 Blind

Striegel, Jana. *Homeroom Exercise.* Holiday House, 2002. ISBN 0-8234-1579-1 Gr. 4–6 Pediatric Rheumatoid Arthritis

Trueman, Terry. *Cruise Control.* HarperCollins, 2004. ISBN 0-06-623960-5 Gr. 6 & up Profoundly Disabled

Wilson, Dawn. *Saint Jude.* Tudor, 2000. ISBN 0-936389-68-0 Young Adult Bipolar Disorder

Winkler, Henry. *Niagara Falls, or Does It?* Penguin Group, 2003. ISBN 0-448-43232-3 Gr. 3–7 Learning Disability

Winkler, Henry, and Lin Oliver. *Holy Enchilada.* Penguin Group, 2004. ISBN 0-448-43554-3 Gr. 3–7 Learning Disability

## Picture Books

Lester, Helen. *Hooway for Wodney Wat.* Houghton Mifflin, 1999. ISBN 0-395-92392-1 Gr. PK–3 Speech Impediment

Millman, Isaac. *Moses Goes to a Concert.* Farrar, Straus & Giroux, 1998. ISBN 0-374-35067-1 Gr. PS–3 Deaf

_____. *Moses Goes to School.* Farrar, Straus & Giroux, 2000. ISBN 0-374-35069-8 Gr. 0–3 Deaf

Polacco, Patricia. *Thank You, Mr. Falker.* Penguin Group, 2001. ISBN 0-399-23732-1 Gr. PK & up Learning Disability

Rau, Dana Meachen. *The Secret Code.* Scholastic, 1998. ISBN 0-516-20700-8 Gr. K–2 Blind

Shriver, Maria. *What's Wrong with Timmy?* Little, Brown and Company, 2001. ISBN 0-316-23337-4 Gr. PS–3 Mental Retardation

Stewart, Shannon. *Sea Crow.* Orca Book Publishers, 2004. ISBN 1-55143-288-9 Gr. PS–3 Prosthetic

Strom, Maria Diaz. *Rainbow Joe and Me.* Lee & Low, 2002. ISBN 1-58430-050-7 Gr. PK–3 Blind

## Nonfiction

Edwards, Nicola. *My Friend Is Blind.* Chrysalis Education, 2004. ISBN 1-59389-170-9 Juvenile

Hale, Natalie. *Oh Brother! Growing Up with a Special Needs Sibling.* American Psychological Association, 2004. ISBN 1-59147-061-7 Juvenile

Kent, Deborah. *Athletes with Disabilities.* Scholastic Library, 2003. ISBN 0-531-12019-8 Juvenile

McMahon, Patricia. *Summer Tunes: A Martha's Vineyard Vacation.* Boyds Mills, 2003. ISBN 1-56397-572-6 Gr. 4–6 Physically Disabled

Powell, Jillian. *Sam Uses a Wheelchair.* Facts On File, 2004. ISBN 0-7910-8180-X Gr. 2–4

## Series

*Coping.* Rosen Publishing Group, 2005. ISBN 1-4042-0226-9 (11 titles) Gr. 7–12

*Disabilities.* Scholastic/Franklin Watts, ISBN 0-531-17447-6 (3 titles) Gr. 5–7

# Discussion Questions

- Has more exposure to people with exceptionalities made you more compassionate?

- Do you see more people with exceptionalities in the workplace? In school?

- Does reading and learning about various exceptionalities help you to be more understanding?

- Does knowing more about individual exceptionalities helps us to be more accommodating?

- Do stars and celebrities with exceptionalities make us more aware of what it is like to live with a disability?

# Featured Author

## Patricia Polacco

**Birthplace:** Lansing, Michigan
**Date of Birth:** 1944
**Current Home:** Union City, Michigan
**Titles**

*Rotten Richie and the Ultimate Dare* (2006)

*Something About Hensley's* (2006)

*Emma Kate* (2005)

*The Graves Family Goes Camping* (2005)

*Mommies Say Shh!* (2005)

*John Phillip Duck* (2004)

*Oh, Look!* (2004)

*An Orange for Frankie* (2004)

*The Graves Family* (2003)

*Christmas Tapestry* (2002)

*When Lightning Comes in a Jar* (2002)

*Betty Doll* (2001)

*Mr. Lincoln's Way* (2001)

*The Butterfly* (2000)

*Luba and the Wren* (1999)

*Welcome, Comfort* (1999)

*Thank You, Mr. Falker* (1998)

*Mrs. Mack* (1998)

*In Enzo's Splendid Gardens* (1997)

*Aunt Chip and the Great Triple Creek Dam Affair* (1996)

*I Can Hear the Sun: A Modern Myth* (1996)

*The Trees of the Dancing Goats* (1996)

*Babushka's Mother Goose* (1995)

*My Ol' Man* (1995)

*My Rotten Redheaded Older Brother* (1994)

*Pink and Say* (1994)

## Interesting Information

- Patricia didn't learn to read until she was fourteen.

- She has dyslexia.

- She did not start writing children's book until she was forty-one years old.

**Web site:** http://www.patriciapolacco.com

**Contact:** For personal questions or comments: Traci Polacco, Events Coordinator and Personal Assistant, email: spolacco@net-link.net

# Annotated Journal Article

Moore, Michele. "Meeting the Educational Needs of Young Gifted Readers in the Regular Classroom." *Gifted Child Today Magazine* (October 2005): 40.

Gifted readers are known to utilize effective reading strategies and push themselves to read any text. It is difficult to find advanced-level books with age-appropriate material. The article features a long list of suggested components in any program for gifted readers. As much as half of the grade-level curriculum for these students could be eliminated. Renzulli's triad enrichment model is featured and suggested for use with these gifted readers.

# Resources

## Books

Carter, Alden. *Stretching Ourselves: Kids with Cerebral Palsy.* Albert Whitman, 2000. ISBN 0-8075-7637-9

Harry, Beth and Janette K. Klingner. *Why Are So Many Minority Students in Special Education?: Understanding Race and Disability in Schools.* Teachers College Press, 2006. ISBN 0-8077-4624-X

Zysk, Veronica, and Ellen Notbohm. *1001 Great Ideas for Teaching and Raising Children with Autism Spectrum Disorders.* Future Horizons, 2004. ISBN 1-932565-19-1

## Organizations

Council for Exceptional Children
1111 North Glebe Road Suite 300
Arlington, VA 22201-5704

American Foundation for the Blind
11 Penn Plaza, Suite 300
New York, NY 10001

United Cerebral Palsy
1660 L Street, NW, Suite 700
Washington, DC 20036

American Association on Mental Retardation
444 North Capitol Street, NW, Suite 846
Washington, D.C. 20001-1512

National Association for Gifted Children
1707 L Street, NW, Suite 550
Washington, DC 20036

## Web Sites

**American Foundation for the Blind:** http://www.afb.org/

**Alexander Graham Bell Association for the Deaf and hard of Hearing:** http://www.agbell.org/DesktopDefault.aspx

**National Dissemination Center for Children with Disabilities:** http://www.nichcy.org/

**United Cerebral Palsy:** http://www.ucp.org/

**United Spinal Association:** http://www.unitedspinal.org/

**American Association on Mental Retardation:** http://www.aamr.org

**Council for Exceptional Children:** http://www.cec.sped.org

**Autism Society of America:** http://www.autism-society.org/site/PageServer

**National Down Syndrome Society:** http://www.ndss.org/

**The International Dyslexia Association:** http://www.interdys.org/

**National Association for Gifted Children:** http://www.nacg.org

**LD (Learning Disabilities) Online:** http://www.ldonline.org

**Additude:** http://www.additudemag.com

**Mobility International USA:** http://www.miusa.org

**The National Information Center for Children and Youth with Disabilities:** http://nichcy.org

# Award

## Schneider Family Book Award

The Schneider Family Book Awards honor an author or illustrator for a book that embodies an artistic expression of the disability experience for child and adolescent audiences. The book must portray some aspect of living with a disability or that of a friend or family member, whether the disability is physical, mental, or emotional.

Schneider Family Book Award Recipients 2005

### *Young Children's Book*

Bertrand, Diane Gonzales. *My Pal Victor/Mi Amigo, Victor.*

### *Middle School Book*

Ryan, Pam Muñoz. *Becoming Naomi León.*

### *Teen Book*

Abeel, Samantha. *My Thirteenth Winter: A Memoir.*

# Chapter 13

# Gender

## Introduction

In 1972, Title IX of the Education Amendments to the Civil Rights Act of 1964, banned sex discrimination in schools in all aspect—from academics to athletics. The main idea was to allow equal funding for girls' sports, which had often been forgotten in favor of boys' sports. Then, in 1973, Marlo Thomas recorded an album and had a TV show called *Free to Be You and Me,* which encouraged kids to be themselves and not worry about gender stereotypes. Today we are seeing a focus on boys and their educational issues; it seems that girls are in the lead and boys are falling behind.

Many of the current picture books and realistic fiction stories tell about single moms raising families, going to school, starting businesses, and making their own decisions. It seems today that there isn't anything girls and women can't do. The literature selected here reflects this trend.

## Definition

**Gender:** Sexual identity, especially in relation to society or culture. (http://www.dictionary.com)

# Annotations

Bauer, Cat. *Harley, Like a Person.* Winslow Press, 2000. ISBN 1-890817-48-1 Gr. 7 & up
Fourteen-year-old Harley is certain that she has been adopted. She lives in a dysfunctional family with an alcoholic, abusive father and a helpless mother. She has different colored eyes than her parents, she finds a discrepancy in her birth certificate, and she is talented in art and poetry, unlike either of her parents. She finds a note and matches the information with her mother's high school yearbook and sets off to find her real father and make changes in her life.

Munsch, Robert. *Paper Bag Princess.* Annick Press, 1986. ISBN 0-920236-25-1 Gr. PS–2
Princess Elizabeth is planning her wedding to Prince Ronald when a dragon attacks the castle and kidnaps Ronald. So Elizabeth goes off and finds the dragon, outsmarts him, and finally rescues Ronald. But Ronald is not too happy to see Princess Elizabeth looking dirty and disheveled. Then doesn't he get a surprise!

O'Malley, Kevin. *Once upon a Cool Motorcycle Dude.* Walker & Company, 2005. ISBN 0-8027-8947-1 Gr. 1–4
For a library project, a boy and a girl had to tell their favorite fairy tale. They could mot agree on one, so they just made one up. The girl started with a castle and a princess who had eight ponies, and as she was naming them, the boy jumped in and told how a giant came and stole one of the ponies. The girl said that the rest of the ponies and the princess cried, and each night the giant returned to take ponies until only one was left. The boy then told of a cool muscle dude who rode up to the castle on a motorcycle and promised to guard the last pony if the king would give him the gold thread that the princess makes. On and on the story goes as the boy and girl tell it from their points of view.

Pattison, Darcy. *19 Girls and Me.* Philomel, 2006. ISBN 0-399-24336-4 Juvenile
John Hercules Po's kindergarten class consists of nineteen girls and one boy—John Hercules. His older brother warns that all those girls will make John Hercules a sissy. But John Hercules says he will turn the girls into tomboys. The girls amaze John Hercules with the things they are willing and able to do. In the end, John Hercules tells his brother he has nineteen *friends*!

Van Draanen, Wendelin. *Flipped.* Random House, 2003. ISBN 0-375-82544-4 Gr. 5–9
This same story is told alternately from the viewpoints of Bryce and then Juli. It all starts when Bryce moves into the neighborhood and Juli anxiously awaits his arrival. Bryce's father immediately thinks she is a pest, and Bryce agrees. Bryce does everything to avoid Juli. But Juli is not afraid to speak her mind, and she sits in a beloved sycamore tree when the owner tries to cut it down. After Juli appears in the paper supporting her cause, Bryce's grandfather becomes interested in her because Juli reminds him of his deceased wife. Bryce begins to look at Juli in a new way at the same time Juli sees through Bryce's shallowness. Each grows in their own way, and the journey is delightful.

# Bibliography

Anderson, Laura Halse. *Prom.* Penguin Group, 2006. ISBN 0-14-240570-1 Young Adult

_____. *Speak.* Farrar, Straus & Giroux, 1999. ISBN 0-374-37152-0 Young Adult

Castelucci, Cecil. *Boy Proof.* Candlewick Press, 2005. ISBN 0-7636-2333-4 Gr. 7–10

Cirrone, Dorian. *Dancing in the Red Shoes.* HarperCollins, 2005. ISBN 0-06-0550702-8 Gr. 7–10

Fitzgerald, Dawn. *Getting in the Game.* Roaring Brook Press. 2005. ISBN 1-59643-044-3 Gr. 4–7

Goobie, Beth. *Sticks and Stones.* Orca Book Publishers, 2002. ISBN 1-55143-213-7 Young Adult (for mature readers)

Lantz, Francess Lin. *The Day Joanie Frankenhouser Became a Boy.* Dutton, 2005. ISBN 0-525-47437-4 Gr. 4–7

Mackler, Carolyn. *The Earth, My Butt, and Other Big Round Things.* Candlewick Press, 2003. ISBN 0-7636-1958-2 Young Adult

Naylor, Phyllis Reynolds. *Simply Alice.* Atheneum, 2002. ISBN 0-689-82635-4 Gr. 7–10

Nelson, Blake. *Prom Anonymous.* Penguin Group, 2006. ISBN 0-670-05945-5 Young Adult

Ryan, Pam Muñoz. *Becoming Naomi León.* Scholastic, 2004. ISBN 0-439-26969-5 Gr. 4–7

Smith, Sherri L. *Lucy the Giant.* Delacorte, 2002. ISBN 0-385-72940-5 Gr. 7–10

Testa, Maria. *Some Kind of Pride.* Delacorte, 2001. ISBN 0-385-32782-X Gr. 3–6

## Picture Books

Bunting, Eve. *Girls A to Z.* Boyds Mills, 2002. ISBN 1-56397-147-X Gr. PS–2

Funke, Cornelia. *The Princess Knight.* Scholastic, 2004. ISBN 0-439-53630-8 Gr. K–3

Geeslin, Campbell. *Elena's Serenade.* Atheneum, 2004. ISBN 0-689-84908-7 Gr. PS–2

Hill, Susanna Leonard. *Punxsutawney Phyllis.* Holiday House, 2005. ISBN 0-8234-1872-3 9 Gr. PS–2

Kroll, Virginia L. *Girl, You're Amazing!* Albert Whitman, 2001. ISBN 0-8075-2930-3 Gr. 0-4

McClintock, Barbara. *Dahlia.* Farrar, Straus & Girroux, 2002. ISBN 0-374-31678-3 Gr. PS–2

Newman, Leslea. *A Fire Engine for Ruthie.* Clarion, 2004. ISBN 0-618-15989-4 Gr. PS–2

Plourde, Lynne. *School Picture Day.* Penguin Group, 2002. ISBN 0-525-46886-2 Gr. K–3

Willis, Jeanne. *I Want to Be a Cowgirl.* Henry Holt, 2002. ISBN 0-8050-6997-6 Gr. PS–2

## Nonfiction

Borden, Sarah, and Sarah Miller. *Middle School: How to Deal.* Chronicle Books, 2005. ISBN 0-8118-4497-0 Juvenile

MacDonald, Fiona. *Equal Opportunities.* Whitecap Books, 2006. ISBN 1-55285-744-1 Gr. 4–12

Rice, Ashley. *You Are an Amazing Girl: A Very Special Book About Being You and Making Your Dreams Come True.* Blue Mountain Arts, 2006. ISBN 1-59842-066-6 Juvenile

Schwager, Tina, and Michele Schuerger. *Cool Women, Hot Jobs ... And How You Can Go for It, Too!* Free Spirit, 2004. ISBN 1-57542-109-7 Gr. 6 & up

## Series

*Women's Adventures in Science.* 10 titles. Scholastic/Franklin Watts, 2005. ISBN 0-531-16824-7 Gr. 7–9

*Women Who Win.* Chelsea House, 2005. 12 titles. ISBN 0-7910-6731-9 Gr. 4–12

# Discussion Questions

- Are both genders treated equally in schools?

- Why is it necessary to have laws (Title IX) that ensure females equal access to sports? Should girls be allowed to play all sports?

- Should females be allowed to pursue careers in fields traditionally dominated by males?

- Should females be treated fairly and equitable in all careers and in top positions?

- Is there too much focus on women now? Not enough?

# Featured Author

## Wendelin Van Draanen

**Birthplace:** Chicago, IL
**Date of Birth:** January 6
**Current Home:** Santa Maria, California
**Titles**

*Runaway* (2006)

*Sammy Keyes and the Dead Giveaway* (2005)

*Shredderman: Enemy Spy* (2005)

*Shredderman: Meet the Gecko* (2005)

*Sammy Keyes and the Psycho Kitty Queen* (2004)

*Shredderman: Attack of the Tagger* (2004)

*Shredderman: Secret Identity* (2004)

*Sammy Keyes and the Art of Deception* (2003)

*Swear to Howdy* (2003)

*Sammy Keyes and the Search for Snake Eyes* (2002)

*Flipped* (2001)

*Sammy Keyes and the Curse of Moustache Mary* (2001)

*Sammy Keyes and the Hollywood Mummy* (2001)

*Sammy Keyes and the Skeleton Man* (2001)

*Sammy Keyes and the Runaway Elf* (1999)

*Sammy Keyes and the Sisters of Mercy* (1999)

*How I Survived Being a Girl* (1998)

*Sammy Keyes and the Hotel Thief* (1998)

**Interesting Information**

- Growing up, Van Draanen was a tomboy who loved to be outside chasing down adventure.

- Her mother taught her to read at an early age.

- Her hobbies include the "Three R's": Reading, Running, and Rock 'n' Roll.

**Web Site:** http://www.randomhouse.com/kids/vandraanen/

**Contact:**
c/o Children's Publicity
Random House
1745 Broadway
New York, NY 10019

# Annotated Journal Articles

Pinsonneault, Susan, and Kara Malhi. "How Can Teachers Support Gender Equity in Their Classrooms?" *Educational Insights* (Volume 8, Number 3, 2003).

These authors encourage teachers to select books that portray people in a variety of roles who come from different backgrounds. The authors found that males are most often the protagonists in books, so they endeavored to find titles with female protagonists as well. Teachers should also be aware of the needs and interests of their students so that they select books that will allow their students to make valuable and necessary connections.

Singh, Manjari. "Gender Issues in Children's Literature." *Eric Digest*, ED424591 98.

It is important to be aware of how gender roles are portrayed in children's books. Gender bias appears often. Male main characters are represented twice as many times as females. Many books represent common stereotypical roles for males and females. The articles suggest that adults teach respect for both genders, that the reactions of characters depend on the situation and not the gender, that achievements and occupations should be gender free, and that it is important to validate both males and females.

# Resources

## Books

Friedman, Ellen, and Jennifer Marshall. *Issues of Gender.* Longman, 2003. ISBN 0-321-10879-5

Kesselman, Amy. *Women: Images & Realities, A Multicultural Anthology.* McGraw-Hill, 2002. ISBN 0-07-312764-7

## Organizations

American Association of University Women
1111 Sixteenth St. N.W.
Washington, DC 20036

## Web Sites

**Kaye Vandergrift's Gender and Culture in Picture Books:** http://www.scils.rutgers.edu/~kvander/Culture/index.html

**National Education Association—Title IX Resources:** http://www.nea.org/titlenine/resources-titlenine.html

**American Association of University Women:** http://www.aauw.org/

**National Museum of Women in the Arts:** http://www.nmwa.org/

**Distinguished Women of Past and Present:** http://www.distinguishedwomen.com/

**Webgrrls International:** http://www.webgrrls.com/

**Girl Start: Smart from the Start:** http://www.girlstart.com/

**Dads and Daughters:** http://www.dadsanddaughters.org/

**Women's Educational Equity:** http://www.edc.org/WomensEquity

**Women's College Coalition:** http://www.academic.org

# Chapter *14*

# Sexual Orientation

## Introduction

Since colonial times, people have been persecuted (even sentenced to death) for their sexual orientation. Scientifically speaking, we know more about sexual orientation now than we ever did in the past. Leonard Sax, a medical doctor and a psychologist, in his book, *Why Gender Matters: What Parents and Teachers Need to Know About the Emerging Science of Sex Differences* (2005), makes some very clear statements. This analogy is clearest: "Some children are destined at birth to be left-handed, and some boys are destined at birth to grow up to be gay."

Despite the scientific support, gays who "come out" often have a difficult time. They are called names and subjected to all sorts of physical violence, from beatings to murder. Many Americans believe that homosexuality is wrong and that homosexuals can simply refuse to be that way. This makes it extremely difficult for children in gay families and for children and young adults struggling with homosexual feelings.

## Definition

**Sexual Orientation:** *Gay* refers to men whose primary attraction is to other men. *Lesbian* refers to women whose primary attraction is to other women. *Bisexual* refers to men or women whose attraction is to both sexes. *Transsexual* or *transgender* refers to men or women whose physical characteristics place them in one gender group yet emotionally they identify with another. (Magazine Publishers of America)

# Annotations

De Haan, Linda, and Stern Nijland. *King & King.* Tricycle, 2002. ISBN 1-58246-061-2 Gr. PS–3
   Delightful illustrations depict a royal family with a son of marriageable age. His mother, the queen, decides that it is high time that her son takes a wife, and so she invites eligible princesses from far and wide so the he can make a choice. One after another they are introduced to the prince, but he shows no interest. Finally, he takes a liking to the brother of one of the princesses. The family accepts his choice and the two princes become a couple and eventually, king and king!

Howe, James. *Totally Joe.* Atheneum, 2005. ISBN 0-689-83957-X Gr. 5 & up
   Joe Bunch's assignment for the year is to write an alphabiography. During that year he turns thirteen, is OUT to his family and friends, celebrates No-Name Day by no longer being a victim of Kevin Hennessey, and becomes "Totally Joe"—or comfortable with himself. Others in the story are not ready to admit they are gay, but Joe knows that being gay is not a choice but who you are. Even though Joe runs out of letters, this is a story that must be continued.

Levithan, David. *Boy Meets Boy.* Knopf, 2003. ISBN 0-375-92400-0 Gr. 7 & up
   From an early age, Paul has known that he is gay. When he was in the third grade, he ran for the president of his class as a gay candidate. His other friends have not been as lucky. Tony has to keep his true identify a secret because of his parents' religious convictions. Kyle is lost and has feelings for both boys and girls. This book is about Paul's relationship with each of his individual friends. Paul makes some mistakes, but he bravely shows his friends how he feels.

Sanchez, Alex. *So Hard to Say.* Simon & Schuster, 2004. ISBN 0-689-86564-3 Juvenile
   Frederick, thirteen years old, reluctantly moves away from his friends in Wisconsin to California. He meets Xio, who is Mexican American. Gradually they become good friends, but Xio wants to be more than friends, and Frederick is confused because he does not feel the same. Frederick comes to terms with the reality that he may be gay, and Xio learns to accept Frederick as he is. Even though they may not have a sexual relationship, their friendship is recognized and valued.

# Bibliography

Alphin, Elaine Marie. *Simon Says.* Harcourt Brace, 2002. ISBN 0-15-216355-7 Gr. 7 & up

Anshaw, Carol. *Lucky in the Corner: A Novel.* Houghton Mifflin, 2002. ISBN 0-618-34070-X General Adult

Boock, Paula. *Dare Truth or Promise.* Houghton Mifflin, 1999. ISBN 0-395-97117-9 Gr. 7–12

Coville, Bruce. *The Skull of Truth.* Harcourt Brace, 1997. ISBN 0-15-275457-1 Gr. 3–7

Ferris, Jean. *Eight Seconds.* Harcourt Brace, 2002. ISBN 0-15-202367-4 Young Adult

Freyman-Weyr, Garret. *My Heartbeat.* Houghton Mifflin, 2002. ISBN 0-618-14181-2 Young Adult

Garden, Nancy. *Molly's Secret.* Farrar, Straus & Giroux, 2000. ISBN 0-374-33273-0 Gr. 3–7

Hall, John. *Is He or Isn't He?* Morrow/Avon, 2006. ISBN 0-06-078747-3 Juvenile

Hartinger, Brent. *Geography Club*. Harper Tempest, 2002. ISBN 0-06-001223-4 Gr. 8 & up

_____. *The Order of the Poison Oak*. Harper Tempest, 2005. ISBN 0-06-056730-9 Gr. 8 & up

Jenkins, A. M. *Breaking Boxes*. Delacorte Books for Young Readers, 1997. ISBN 0-606-17834-1 Gr. 7–10

Kerr, M. E. *"Hello" I Lied*. HarperCollins, 1997. ISBN 0-06-027529-4 Gr. 10 & up

Koertge, Ronald. *Boy Girl Boy*. Harcourt, 2005. ISBN 0-15-205325-3 Young Adult

Koja, Kathe. *Talk*. Thorndike Press, 2006. ISBN 0-7862-8811-3 Young Adult

LaRochelle, David. *Absolutely, Positively Not*. Scholastic, 2005. ISBN 0-439-59109-0 Young Adult

Levithan, David, and Billy Merrell, eds. *The Full Spectrum: A New Generation of Writing About Gay, Lesbian, Bisexual, Transgender, Questioning, and Other Identities*. Knopf, 2006. ISBN 0-375-83290-4 Gr. 7 & up

Myracle, Lauren. *Kissing Kate*. Penguin, 2004. ISBN 0-14-240241-9 Gr. 9 & up

Papademetriou, Lisa. *M or F?* Penguin, 2005. ISBN 1-59514-034-4 Gr. 3–7

Peters, Julia Anne. *Keeping You Secret*. Little, Brown and Company, 2003. ISBN 0-316-00985-7 Gr. 9 & up

_____. *Luna*. Little, Brown and Company, 2006. ISBN 0-316-01127-4 Gr. 5 & up

Ryan, Sara. *Empress of the World*. Viking, 2001. ISBN 0-670-89688-8 Gr. 7 & up

Sanchez, Alex. *Getting It*. Simon & Schuster, 2006. ISBN 1-4169-0896-X Young Adult

_____. *Rainbow Road*. Simon & Schuster, 2005. ISBN 0-0689-86565-1 Gr. 8 & up

Wersba, Barbara. *Whistle Me Home*. Henry Holt, 1997. ISBN 0-8050-4850-2 Gr. 9 & up

Winick, Judd. *Pedro and Me*. Henry Holt, 2000. ISBN 0-8050-6403-6 Gr. 7 & up

Withrow, Sarah. *Box Girl*. Groundwood Books, 2002. ISBN 0-88899-436-2 Gr. 5–8

Wittlinger, Ellen. *Hard Love*. Simon & Schuster, 1999. ISBN 0-689-82134-4 Young Adult

Woodson, Jacqueline. *Behind You*. Putnam, 2004. ISBN 0-399-23988-X Gr. 8 & up

_____. *The House You Pass on the Way*. Delacorte, 1997. ISBN 0-385-32189-9 Young Adult

Yamanaka, Lois Ann. *Name Me Nobody*. Sagebrush Education Resources, 2000. ISBN 0-613-31521-9 Gr. 7 & up

## Picture Books

Aldrich, Andrew. *How My Family Came to Be: Daddy, Papa and Me*. New Family Press, 2003. ISBN 0-9742008-0-8 Juvenile

De Haan, Linda, and Stern Nijland. *King & King & Family*. Tricycle, 2004. ISBN 1-58246-113-9 Gr. PS–3

Garden, Nancy. *Molly's Family*. Farrar, Straus & Giroux, 2004. ISBN 0-374-35002-7 Gr. PS–2

Gonzalez, Rigoberto. *Antonio's Card*. Children's Book Press, 2005. ISBN 0-89239-204-5 Juvenile

Newman, Leslea. *Felicia's Favorite Story.* Two Lives, 2003. ISBN 0-9674468-5-6 Gr. PS–3

_____. *Heather Has Two Mommies.* Alyson Publications, 2000. ISBN 1-55583-543-0 Gr. PS–3

Richardson, Justin, and Peter Parnell. *And Tango Makes Three.* Simon & Schuster, 2005. ISBN 0-689-87845-1 Gr. PS & up

Setterington, Ken. *Mom and Mum Are Getting Married.* Second Story Press, 2004. ISBN 1-896764-84-3 Gr. PS–5

## Nonfiction

Endersbe, Julie. *Homosexuality: What Does It Mean?* Capstone Press, 1999. ISBN 0-7368-0275-4 Gr. 4–6

Greenberg, Keith Elliot. *Zack's Story: Growing Up with Same-Sex Parents.* Carolrhoda Books, 1996. ISBN 0-8225-2581-X Gr. 2–4

Marcovitz, Hal. *Teens and Gay Issues.* Mason Crest, 2005. ISBN 1-59084-873-X Gr. 7–9

Mastoon, Adam. *The Shared Heart: Portraits and Stories Celebrating Lesbian, Gay, and Bisexual Young People.* HarperCollins, 2001. ISBN 0-06-29556-2 Young Adult

Snow, Edith. *How It Feels to Have a Gay or Lesbian Parent: A Book by Kids for Kids of All Ages.* Haworth Press, 2004. ISBN 1-56023-420-2 Juvenile

## Series

*Gay and Lesbian Writers.* Six titles. Chelsea House, 2005. ISBN 0-7910-8477-9 Middle/High School

# Discussion Questions

- In general, are we accepting of people with sexual orientation different from ours? Why or why not?

- Do the students in your school accept these students for who they are? Who is the most accepting?

- Are there others in your school or community who are afraid to "come out"? If so, what might happen to them? What do they fear?

- Scientists tell us that sexual orientation is not a choice. Do you think all people will ever accept that? What will it take for people to be accepting?

# Featured Author

## David Levithan

**Birthplace:** Short Hills, NJ
**Date of Birth:** September 2, 1972
**Current Home:** Hoboken, NJ
**Titles**

> *Wide Awake* (2006)
>
> *Nick and Norah's Infinite Playlist* (2006)
>
> *The Full Spectrum: A New Generation of Writing About Gay, Lesbian, Bisexual, Transgender, Questioning, and Other Identities* (2006)
>
> *Are We There Yet?* (2005)
>
> *Marly's Ghost* (2005)
>
> *The Realm of Possibility* (2004)
>
> *Boy Meets Boy* (2003)

**Interesting Information**

- Editor for the PUSH imprint at Scholastic in Manhattan

- Graduate of Brown University

- *Realm of Possibility* won the American Library Association's Best Books for Young Adults Award in 2005

**Web Site:** http://www.davidlevithan.com

**Contact Information:** david@davidlevithan.com

# Annotated Journal Articles

Herbeck, Joyce. "Creating a Safe Learning Environment: Books for Young People about Homosexuality." *Book Links* (January 2002): 30–34.

> Gay students often hear negative comments; experience verbal, emotional, and physical abuse; and are two to six times more likely to attempt to commit suicide than other youth. This article features a list of novels, collections, and nonfiction titles to help educate all students about homosexuality and to help teachers and librarians create an environment free from hate and harassment.

King, Kevin A. R. "Author Visits or Hobnobbing with the Semi-Rich and Literate." *VOYA* (February 2006): 470–73.

> David Levithan was the featured author for "Get Real @ Your Library" celebration for Teen Read Week at the Kalamazoo Public Library in Michigan. The author tells about how he set up the visit and all the things he did to make the visit go smoothly. David spoke about his book *Boy Meets Boy* because the issue to be discussed that week was the GLBTQ Teen. During one of the presentations, there were some protestors picketing outside, and David was interviewed by the local TV station. He handled the situation extremely well and spoke eloquently about the rights of all people. The visit was very successful and informative for all involved.

Owens, Tom. "Totally James." *Teaching Tolerance* (spring 2006): 19–23.

> This article is an interview with author, James Howe, who has recently shared that he is gay. *The Misfits* and *Totally James* are his recent titles with gay main characters. He discusses his life, how his "coming out" has changed him, and how he deals with speaking to middle and high school students.

Whelan, Debra Lau. "Out and Ignored: Why Are So Many School Libraries Reluctant to Embrace Gay Teens?" *School Library Journal* (January 2006): 46–50.

> The article presents statistics about the number of gays in middle and high schools and the serious lack of fiction and nonfiction information available for them. It may be a reflection of the community, national politics, the librarians, the school board, or other issues. Many lives are touched by these issues and it is important to realize that this is an important aspect of human life. This group of young people needs to be supported and assisted as we would help any other group.

# Resources

## Books

Ressler, Paula. *Dramatic Changes: Talking About Sexual Orientation and Gender Identity with High School Students Through Drama.* Heinemann, 2002. ISBN 0-325-00414-5

Stevenson, Michael, and Jeanine C. Cogan. *Everyday Activism: A Handbook for Lesbian, Gay and Bisexual People and Their Allies Get Active, Know the Issues, Join the Fight, Make a Difference!* Routledge, 2003. ISBN 0-415-94481-3

## Organizations

National Gay and Lesbian Task Force
1325 Massachusetts Ave. NW, Suite 600
Washington, DC 20005

Parents and Friends of Lesbians and Gays
1726 M Street, NW, Suite 400
Washington, DC 20036

## Web Sites

**National Gay and Lesbian Task Force:** http://www.ngltf.org/main.html

**Parents and Friends of Lesbians and Gays:** http://wwwpflag.org

**Gay, Lesbian, and Straight Education Network:** http://www.glsen.org/cgi-bin/iowa/home.html

**Rainbow Reading: Gay and Lesbian Characters and Themes in Children's Books:** http://www.armory.com/~web/gaybooks.html

**Young Gay America:** http://www.younggayamerica.com/

**Alex Sanchez:** http://www.alexsanchez.com.

**Human Rights Campaign's Family Net:** http://www.hrc.org/familynet/index.asp

**Children of Lesbians and Gays Everywhere:** http://www.colage.org

**Family Pride Coalition:** http://www.familypride.org

# Chapter *15*

# Socioeconomic Status

## Introduction

Americans, who live in the wealthiest nation in the world, do not like to believe that there are families here who cannot afford basic necessities. Over 17 percent of all children (about 13 million) nationwide live in poverty. Poverty is defined as having a total income below 17,000 for a family of three. About 6 million children live in families with a total income of under $9,000 for a family of three. Poverty is especially prevalent in black and Latino families and in families with immigrant parents. Poverty hinders a child's ability to learn and reason.

## Definition

**Socioeconomic status:** of, pertaining to, or signifying the combination or interaction of social and economic factors; the state or condition of having little or no money, goods, or means of support; condition of being poor; indigence. (http://www.dictionary.com)

# Annotations

Strasser, Todd. *Can't Get There from Here.* Simon & Schuster, 2004. ISBN 0-689-84169-8 Young Adult

> A girl named Maybe lives on the streets of New York City with other homeless teens. Life is very difficult, and friends are dying of hunger, disease, and drugs. A new girl, named Tears, joins the group, and Maybe decides to try to help her get off the streets before they all die.

Van Draanen, Wendelin. *Runaway.* Random House, 2006. ISBN 0-375-83522-9 Gr. 5–8

> Holly's mother has died of an overdose, and Holly is forced to stay in foster homes. At twelve years old, she decides she has had enough and sets off on her own to live on the streets and try to make a better life for herself.

Wolff, Virginia Euwer. *Make Lemonade.* Sagebrush Education Resources, 1994. ISBN 0-7857-3546-1 Young Adult

> Fourteen-year-old LaVaughn lives in the projects with her mother. She takes a babysitting job for the two children of seventeen-year-old Jolly, a single-parent who is unskilled, illiterate, and jobless. LaVaughn encourages her to go back to school, try to make something of herself, and get out of the squalor and poverty with her kids.

Wyeth, Sharon Dennis. *Something Beautiful.* Random House, 2002. ISBN 0-440-41210-2 Gr. 2–4

> A little girl lives in a bad neighborhood, and the area around her apartment is filled with graffiti and garbage. At school, her teacher tells her the definition of the word *beautiful,* and she searches around her neighborhood for something beautiful. She finds something beautiful everywhere she goes and in everyone she meets. Then she goes back to her apartment and sweeps and washes the graffiti off the walls and promises to clean it up and make it beautiful.

# Bibliography

Bowsher, Melodie. *My Lost and Found Life.* Bloomsbury, 2006. ISBN 1-58234-736-0 Young Adult

Butcher, Kristin. *The Runaways.* Kids Can Press, 1997. ISBN 1-55074-413-5 Gr. 4–6

Carey, Janet Lee. *The Double Life of Zoe Flynn.* Simon & Schuster, 2004. ISBN 0-689-85604-0 Juvenile

Conly, Jane Leslie. *While No One Was Watching.* Sagebrush Education Resources, 2000. ISBN 0-613-28699-5 Gr. 3–7

Cooley, Beth. *Shelter.* Delacorte, 2006. ISBN 0-385-73330-4 Young Adult

Creel, Ann Howard. *A Ceiling of Stars.* Pleasant Company, 1999. ISBN 1-56247-848-6 Gr. 5 & up

Deuker, Carl. *Runner.* Houghton Mifflin, 2005. ISBN 0-618-54298-1 Young Adult

Easton, Kelly. *Trouble at Betts' Pets.* Candlewick Press, 2002. ISBN 0-7636-1580-3 Gr. 3–7

Evans, Douglas. *So What Do You Do?* Front Street, 1997. ISBN 1-886910-20-0 Gr. 4–6

Fenner, Carol. *The King of Dragons.* Simon & Schuster, 1998. ISBN 0-689-82217-0 Gr. 5–8

_____. *Randall's Wall.* Simon & Schuster, 2000. ISBN 0-689-83558-2 Gr. 4–7

Fogelin, Adrian. *Anna Casey's Place in the World.* Peachtree, 2003. ISBN 1-56145-295-5 Gr. 3–6

Ghent, Natale. *No Small Thing.* Candlewick Press, 2005. ISBN 0-7636-2422-5 Gr. 5–8

Hartnett, Sonya. *Thursday's Child.* Candlewick Press, 2000. ISBN 0-7636-1620-6 Young Adult

Howe, James. *Dew Drop Dead: A Sebastian Barth Mystery.* Simon & Schuster, 2000. ISBN 0-689-80760-2 Gr. 3–7

Hyde, Catherine Ryan. *Becoming Chloe.* Random House, 2006. ISBN 0-375-83258-0 Young Adult

Johnston, Lindsay Lee. *Soul Moon Soup.* Front Street, 2002. ISBN 1-886910-87-1 Gr. 5–7

Koja, Kathe. *The Blue Mirror.* Penguin, 2006. ISNB 0-14-249693-7 Young Adult

Mazer, Norma Fox. *What I Believe.* Harcourt, 2005. ISBN 0-15-201462-4 Gr. 5–9

Myers, Walter Dean. *The Beast.* Scholastic, 2003. ISBN 0-439-36841-3 Juvenile

Sachar, Louis. *Holes.* Random House, 2000. ISBN 0-440-41480-6 Gr. 5–8

Wittlinger, Ellen. *Gracie's Girl.* Simon & Schuster, 2000. ISBN 0-689-82249-9 Gr. 4–7

## Picture Books

Bunting, Eve. *December.* Harcourt, 1997. ISBN 0-15-201434-9 Gr. 1–4

DiSalvo-Ryan, Dyanne. *Uncle Willie and the Soup Kitchen.* HarperCollins, 1997. ISBN 0-688-15285-6 Gr. PS–3

Gunning, Monica. *A Shelter in Our Car.* Children's Book Press, 2004. ISBN 0-89239-189-8 Gr. 1–4

McGovern, Ann. *The Lady in the Box.* Turtle Books, 1997. ISBN 1-890515-01-9 Gr. K–3

McPhail, David. *The Teddy Bear.* Henry Holt, 2002. ISBN 0-8050-6414-1 Gr. K–3

## Nonfiction

Gottfried, Tom. *Homelessness: Whose Problem Is It?* Lerner, 1999. ISBN 0-7613-0953-5 Gr. 7–12

Kowalski, Kathlann. *Poverty in America: Causes and Issues.* Enslow, 2003. ISBN 0-7660-1945-4 Juvenile

Kozol, Jonathan. *Rachel and Her Children: Homeless Families in America.* Crown, 2006. ISBN 0-307-34589-9 General Adult

Mason, Paul. *Poverty.* Heinemann Library, 2005. ISBN 1-4034-7743-4 Juvenile

Stearman, Kaye. *Why Do People Live on the Streets?* Raintree, 2001. ISBN 0-7398-3232-8 Gr. 4–7

# Discussion Questions

- How do students who live in a lower socioeconomic status than their peers deal with differences in their clothing and toys?

- Why does 20 percent of the U.S. population live below the poverty line?

- What can we do at school to eliminate differences and discrimination related to socioeconomic status?

# Featured Author

## Virginia Euwer Wolff

**Birthplace:** Portland, Oregon
**Date of Birth:** 1937
**Current Home:** Oregon City, Oregon
**Titles**

*True Believer* (2001)

*Bat 6* (1998)

*Make Lemonade* (1993)

*The Mozart Season* (1991)

*Probably Still Nick Swanson* (1988)

*Rated PG* (1981)

**Interesting Information**

- Wolff is an accomplished violinist.

- She taught elementary school and high school English.

- She has won numerous awards for her books.

**Contact:**
  c/o Simon & Schuster Children's Publishing
  1230 Avenue of the Americas
  New York, NY 10020

# Annotated Journal Article

Herbeck, Joyce. "Awakening Social Consciousness: Homelessness in Children's Literature." *Book Links* (March 2004): 6–9.

    According to this article, in the United States there are more than 750,000 homeless people, and 38 percent of them are children. It is difficult to get an accurate estimate. The article includes a list of picture books, novels, and nonfiction titles that will raise awareness. There are also some discussion questions. By exposing students to these stories, it is hoped that they will recognize the injustices and issues and help to solve the problem.

# Resources

## Books

Payne, Ruby. *A Framework for Understanding Poverty.* aha! Process, 2005. ISBN 1-929229-48-8

Solley, Bobbie. *When Poverty's Children Write: Celebrating Strengths, Transforming Lives.* Heinemann, 2005. ISBN 0-325-00751-9

## Organizations

Save the Children
2000 M Street NW; Suite 500
Washington D.C. 20036

National Center for Children in Poverty
215 W. 125th Street, 3rd Floor
New York, NY 10027

## Web Sites

**Save the Children USA:** http://www.savethechildren.org/usa/

**National Center for Children in Poverty:** http://www.nccp.org/

**Hearts and Minds—Children in Poverty:** http://www.heartsandminds.org/articles/childpov.htm

# Chapter 16

# Religion

## Introduction

The United States was founded to provide a place for people from Europe who felt they were being persecuted for their religion. Yet some of the Pilgrims arrived here and then proceeded to persecute anyone who did not have the same religious beliefs! We are now a nation of many different religions, and it is against the law to persecute someone because of his or her religion. It seems, however, that not everyone in every American community is tolerant of religions other than their own. Children come to school with many differences: physical, emotional, social, and intellectual. They also bring different cultures and religious practices. We want children to feel safe in our schools, and we want to respect and understand their family beliefs and traditions and rather than work to just tolerate—it is important to understand. Many religions are practiced in the United States, and this is a breakdown based on organized religions in 2001: Christianity 76.5 percent, Judaism 1.3 percent, Islam 0.5 percent, Buddhism 0.5 percent, Hinduism 0.4 percent, and Unitarian Universalism 0.3 percent.

## Definition

**Religion:** a specific fundamental set of beliefs and practices generally agreed upon by a number of persons or sects. (http://www.dictionary.com)

# Annotations

Hautman, Pete. *Godless*. Simon & Schuster, 2005. ISBN 1-4169-0816-1 Gr. 7 & up
> Jason Bock questions the religion of his parents and on a whim forms a new religion, the Church of the Ten-Legged God, formerly known as a water tower. Jason's best friend, Shin, is the First Keeper of the Sacred Test, and he writes as if the water tower is channeling through him. Henry, who is a bully without limits, is named the High Priest because he is the one who can show them the way up the water tower. When Henry slips over the edge of the water tower, the religion begins to dissolve until Jason is the only remaining member.

Ritter, John. *Choosing Up Sides*. Penguin Group, 2000. ISBN 0-698-11840-5 Gr. 5–9
> Luke was the preacher's son of the Holy River Baptizers. His family was sent to Crown Falls on the Ohio River bordering with West Virginia during the 1920s. Luke's father believed "the left side has always been the side of Satan, contrary to God." When Luke was younger, Pa strapped his left arm to his body until it went numb, but it trained him to be right-handed. He was punished any time he used his left hand. One day, Luke stopped to watch a baseball game. The ball rolled to Luke, and he easily threw it back to the bases—left-handed. That pitch changed everything for Luke. He wanted to play ball—to pitch—but he knew that his father thought baseball was nothing but the Devil's playground. Will Luke convince his hot-tempered father that one has to be true to his nature? He learns that it is useless to try to change one's nature just as you cannot turn the great Ohio River around.

Yolen, Jane. *Armageddon Summer*. Harcourt Brace, 1999. ISBN 0-15-202268-6 Gr. 7–12
> Marina and Jed's parents drag them to the mountain retreat of Reverend Beelson to wait for Armageddon—July 27, 2000.

# Bibliography

Blacker, Terence. *The Angel Factory*. Simon & Schuster, 2003. ISBN 0-689-86413-2 Gr. 6–9

Blume, Judy. *Are You There God? It's Me Margaret*. Book Wholesalers, 2000. ISBN 0-7587-9131-3 Gr. 5–7

Brown, Devin. *Not Exactly Normal*. Eerdmans Books, 2005. ISBN 0-8028-5283-1 Gr. 5–8

Carlson, Melody. *My Name Is Chloe: Diary Number 5*. Multnomah, Incorporated, 2003. ISBN 1-59052-018-1 General Adult

Cooper, Ilene. *Sam I Am*. Scholastic, 2006. ISBN 0-439-43968-8 Juvenile

Cormier, Robert. *The Chocolate War*. Random House, 2004. ISBN 0-375-82987-3 Gr. 6–10

Cushman, Karen. *The Loud Silence of Francine Green*. Clarion, 2006. ISBN 0-618-50455-9 Gr. 5–9

Fox, Paula. *One-Eyed Cat*. Simon & Schuster, 2000. ISBN 0-689-83970-7 Gr. 6–9

Gardner, Nancy. *The Year They Burned the Books*. Farrar, Straus & Giroux, 1999. ISBN 0-374-38667-6 Gr. 7 & up

Grimes, Nikki. *Dark Sons*. Hyperion Books, 2005. ISBN 0-7868-1888-3 Gr. 6 & up

Hambrick, Sharon. *Stuart's Run to Faith.* Sagebrush Education Resources, 1999. ISBN 0-613-81775-3 Gr. 3–6

Koja, Kathe. *Buddha Boy.* Farrar, Straus & Giroux, 2003. ISBN 0-374-30998-1 Gr. 6–10

Le Guin, Ursula K. *The Telling.* Penguin Group, 2003. ISBN 0-441-01123-3 General Adult

Levitan, Sonia. *The Singing Mountain.* Simon & Schuster, 2000. ISBN 0-689-83523-X Gr. 8 & up

Littman, Sarah. *Confessions of a Closet Catholic.* Penguin Group, 2006. ISBN 0-14-240597-3 Juvenile

Paulsen, Gary. *The Tent.* Harcourt Children's Books, 2006. ISBN 0-15-205833-8 Young Adult

Ray, Delia. *Singing Hands.* Houghton Mifflin, 2006. ISBN 0-618-65762-2 Gr. 6–9

Rylant, Cynthia. *A Fine White Dust.* Simon & Schuster, 2006. ISBN 1-4169-2769-7 Gr. 5–8

Schmidt, Gary D. *Lizzie Bright and the Buckminster Boy.* Random House, 2006. ISBN 0-553-49495-3 Gr. 5–9

Sumpolec, Sarah Anne. *The Masquerade.* Moody, 2003. ISBN 0-8024-6451-3 Young Adult.

Tolan, Stephanie S. *Save Halloween.* HarperCollins, 1997. ISBN 0-688-15497-2 Gr.5–7

Weaver, Will *Full Service.* Farrar, Straus & Giroux, 2005. ISBN 0-374-32485-9 Gr. 8 & up

Weinheimer, Beckie. *Converting Kate.* Penguin Group, 2007. ISBN 0-670-06152-2 Young Adult

Wittlinger, Ellen. *Blind Faith.* Simon & Schuster, 2006. ISBN 1-4169-0273-2 Gr. 7 & up

## Picture Books

Hawxhurst, Joan C. *Bubbe and Gram: My Two Grandmothers.* Dovetail, 2003. ISBN 0-9651284-2-3 Gr. PS–2

Muth, Jon. *Zen Shorts.* Scholastic, 2005. ISBN 0-439-33911-1 Gr. K–3

Rosen, Michael J. *Elijah's Angel: A Story for Chanukah and Christmas.* Harcourt, 1997. ISBN 0-15-201558-2 Gr. 0 & up

Sasso, Sandy Eisenberg. *God in Between.* Jewish Lights Publishing, 1998. ISBN 1-879045-86-9 Gr. PS–3

Spinelli, Eileen. *City Angel.* Penguin Group, 2004. ISBN 0-8037-2821-2 Gr. PS–2

## Nonfiction

Barnes, Trevor. *The Kingfisher Book of Religion: Festivals, Ceremonies, and Beliefs from Around the World.* Kingfisher, 1999. ISBN 0-753-45199-9 Gr. 6–9

Gellman, Marc, and Thomas Hartman. *How Do You Spell God? Answers to the Big Questions from Around the World.* Morrow, 1995. ISBN 0-688-13041-0 Gr. 5–8

Palmer, Martin, and Elizabeth Breuilly. *Religions of the World: The Illustrated Guide to Origiins,Beliefs, Traditions & Festivals.* Facts on File, 2005. ISBN 0-8160-6258-7 Gr. 8 & up

Loundon, Sumi, ed. *Blue Jean Buddha: Voices of Young Buddhists.* Wisdom Publications, 2001. ISBN 0-86171-177-7 General Adult

Maestro, Betsy. *The Story of Religion.* Clarion, 2006. ISBN 0-395-62364-2 Gr. 0–3

Richmond, Ivan. *Silence and Noise: Growing Up Zen in America.* Simon & Schuster, 2003. ISBN 0-7434-1755-0 General Adult

Shaw, Maura D. *Ten Amazing People: And How They Changed the World.* SkyLight Paths, 2002. ISBN 1-893361-47-0 Gr. 1–5

## Series

*Faith in America.* Chelsea House

*Introduction to the Worls's Major Religions.* Greenwood

*Religion in Focus.* The Creative Company

*Religions of Humanity.* Chelsea House

*Religions of the World.* Chelsea House

*Religions of the World.* Lucent Books/Gale

*World Beliefs and Cultures.* Heinemann Library

*World of Beliefs.* McGraw Hill School Specialty Publishing

# Discussion Questions

- Are people persecuted today in America because of their religion? If so, how?

- Are you tolerant of others in your class or neighborhood that have a different religion than yours? How do you demonstrate that you are tolerant or not?

- Is it important to know something about other religions? Why or why not?

# Featured Author

## Betsy Maestro

**Birthplace:** Brooklyn, New York
**Date of Birth:** January 5, 1944
**Current Home:** Old Lyme, Connecticut
**Titles**

*Liberty or Death: The American Revolution, 1763–1783* (2004)

*The New Americans: Colonial Times: 1620–1689* (2004)

*The Story of Clocks and Calendars* (2004)

*Struggle for a Continent: The French and Indian Wars 1689-1763* (2000)

*The Voice of the People: American Democracy in Action* (1999)

*Geese Find the Missing Piece* (1999)

*Coming to America: The Story of Immigration* (1996)

*The Story of Religion* (1996)

*Exploration and Conquest, the Americans after Columbus: 1500–1620* (1994)

*The Discovery of Americas* (1992)

*The Story of Money* (1989)

*A More Perfect Union: The Story of the Constitution* (1987)

*The Story of the Statue of Liberty* (1986)

**Interesting Information**

- Betsy taught kindergarten and first grade before she started writing.

- Betsy writes the words, and her husband Giulio illustrates their books.

- Betsy and Giulio are known for their nonfiction books and attention to detail.

- Since 1975, Betsy and Giulio have collaborated on more than one hundred books.

**Web Site:** www.maestrobooks.com

**Contact:**
Betsy and Giulio Maestro
74 Mile Creek Road
Old Lyme, CT 06371
(860) 434-9773
Fax: (860) 434-1620
E-mail: bcmaes@aol.com

# Annotated Journal Article

Green, Connie, and Sandra Oldendorf. "Teaching Religious Diversity through Children's Literature." *Childhood Education* (July 2005): 209–12.

With so many children from different backgrounds in our schools today, children easily share information about their special religious activities at home. Others become inquisitive and children's literature is a natural way to learn about different religions. The article does a great job of describing all the major religions, and there is an excellent bibliography of mostly nonfiction titles at the end of the article.

# Resources

## Books

Ellwood, Robert S. *Encyclopedia of World Religions.* Facts on File, 2006. ISBN 0-8160-6141-6

Hopfe, Lewis M. *Religions of the World.* Prentice Hall, 2006. ISBN 0-13-224045-9

Hubbard, Benjamin, John Hatfield, and James Santucci. *An Educator's Classroom Guide to America's Religious Beliefs and Practices.* Libraries Unlimited, 2007. ISBN 156-308-4694

Roof, Wade Clark. *Contemporary American Religion.* Macmillan Reference USA, 2000. ISBN 0-0286-4926-5

## Organizations

National Council of Churches
475 Riverside Drive, Suite 880
New York, NY 10115

International Fellowship of Christians and Jews
30 N. La Salle St., Suite 2600
Chicago, IL 60602-3356

## Web Sites

**Beliefnet:** http://www.beliefnet.com

**Buddha Mind:** http://www.buddhamind.info/

**National Council of Churches:** http://www.ncccusa.org/

**International Fellowship of Christians and Jews:** http://www.ifcj.org/site/PageServer

**Anti-Defamation League:** http://www.adl.org/

**Islamic Council of North America:** http://www.icna.org/icna/index.php

# Works Cited

Bishop, Rudine Sims, ed. *Kaleidoscope: A Multicultural Booklist for Grades K–8*. Urbana, IL: National Council of Teachers of English, 1994.

Brown, Jean E., and Elaine C. Stephens, eds. *United in Diversity: Using Multicultural Young Adult Literature in the Classroom*. Urbana, IL: National Council of Teachers of English, 1998.

Campbell, Patty. "The Sand in the Oyster." *The Horn Book Magazine* (July 1994).

Evans, William, and Julie Topoleski. *The Social and Economic Impact of Native American Casinos*. The Social Science Research Network, 2002.

Hoobler, Dorothy, and Thomas. *We Are Americans: Voices of the Immigrant Experience*. Scholastic Nonfiction, 2003.

Kahlenberg, Richard D. "The New Integration." *Educational Leadership* (May 2006): 22–26.

Kugler, Eileen Gale. "What We Owe Immigrant Children." *Education Week* (May 17, 2006): 32.

Lempke, Susan Dove. "The Faces in the Picture Books." *The Horn Book Magazine* (March/April 1999): 141–47

Meyer, Calvin F., and Elizabeth Kelley Rhoads. "Multiculturalism: Beyond Food, Festival, Folklore, and Fashion." *Kappa Delta Pi Record* (winter 2006): 82–87.

Nikola-Lisa, W. " 'Around My Table' Is Not Always Enough: A Response to Jacqueline Woodson." *The Horn Book Magazine* (May/June 1998): 335–38.

Norton, Donna E. *Multicultural Children's Literature: Through the Eyes of Many Children*. Pearson, 2005.

Sax, Leonard. *Why Gender Matters: What Parents and Teachers Need to Know About the Emerging Science of Sex Differences*. Doubleday, 2005.

Woodson, Jacqueline. "Who Can Tell My Story?" *The Horn Book Magazine* (January/February 1998): 34–38.

# References

Brown, Jean E., and Elaine C. Stephens, eds. *United in Diversity: Using Multicultural Young Adult Literature in the Classroom.* National Council of Teachers of English, 1998.

This book begins with writings by seven authors, then essays by ten students. In the chapters, "Expanding the Curriculum" and "Reflecting Our Lives," nine educators share ways to use multicultural literature paired with various topics and subjects. The appendices include a source guide for locating multicultural literature for young adults and an annotated bibliography.

Corliss, Julia Candace. *Crossing Borders with Literature of Diversity.* Christopher-Gordon, 1998.

This books looks at literature grouped according to various borders: physical, cultural, and inner borders. It covers how to use the literature of diversity through individualized reading, literature circles, thematic units, and challenges. There is a chapter on selecting diverse literature including bias, authenticity, quality, and balance. The appendices group books by theme, culture, and genre.

Gay, Kathlyn. *Cultural Diversity: Conflicts and Challenges: The Ultimate Teen Guide.* Scarecrow Press, 2003.

This is an excellent title for teen and adult reading as it covers all areas of diversity in a straightforward manner. It provides suggestions for making positive changes, describes programs that are working, and offers addresses and Web sites of helpful groups and organizations.

Gilbert, Beverly Boals, and Lina L. Owens. *Cultural Diversity Through Literature: Developing Children's Awareness.* Kaplan Early Learning Company, 2004.

This book is organized by cultural identifier: people of color, region, gender, family, exceptionalities, aged, religion, and work. Each section features five titles. There are several activities for each title.

Jweid, Rosann, and Margaret Rizzo. *Building Character Through Multicultural Literature: A Guide for Middle School Readers.* Scarecrow Press, 2004.

Fifty titles for middle school readers are featured in this book. A framework is followed for each title: awards, characters, character traits, setting, plot, discussion questions, projects, vocabulary, and information about the author. The titles are all organized by culture, and there is a list of useful Web sites at the back of the book.

Norton, Donna E. *Multicultural Children's Literature: Through the Eyes of Many Children.* Pearson, 2005.

This is a literature text for university level classes. It contains an introduction to multicultural literature and then chapters on each: African American, Native American, Latino, Asian, Jewish, and Middle Eastern.

Powell, John. *Encyclopedia of North American Immigration.* Facts on File, 2005.

The author provides information on the historical factors that made immigration necessary, desirable, or possible for the United States and Canada. Data is taken from the 2000 U.S. census and the 2001 Canadian Census, as well recent census for each country. All entries are cross-referenced, concise, and in alphabetical order.

# Annotated Professional Journal Articles

Bainbridge, Joyce, Sylvia Pantaleo, and Monica Ellis. "Multicultural Picture Books: Perspectives from Canada." *The Social Studies* (July/August 1999): 183–86.

    The authors determined that careful selection of multicultural picture books can assist children in understanding a wide variety of diversity issues. These issues can include gender, age, mental disability, and ethnicity. The books can also serve as a springboard for further discussion and research on diversity issues.

Hill, Lynn, Andrew Stremmel, and Victoria Fu. "Teaching Kindness and Compassion in a Diverse World." *Scholastic Early Childhood Today* (November/December 2002): 36–44.

    Beginning with preschool children, it is important to respect and understand differences, languages, books, artifacts, holidays, and family connections by teaching children to work collaboratively. The article lists a variety of resources for teachers and parents.

Kahlenberg, Richard D. "The New Integration." *Educational Leadership* (May 2006): 22–26.

    This article describes the research showing that racial integration does not result in improved achievement. In contrast, socioeconomic integration has a substantial impact on improving achievement for low socioeconomic students regardless of race.

Kugler, Eileen Gale. "What We Owe Immigrant Children." *Education Week* (May 17, 2006): 32.

    Rather than focusing on the services immigrant children require, this article highlights the positives that immigrant children bring to classrooms across the country. The article describes the experiences of Annandale High School students in Virginia. Students learn about the reasons the immigrants are here, they learn differing points of view, and they watch them work hard to achieve a better life for themselves and their families.

Lempke, Susan Dove. "The Faces in the Picture Books." *The Horn Book Magazine* (March/April 1999): 141–47.

    Author-librarian Susan Lempke realized that the 1990s brought a surge in the number of new immigrants coming to the United States. She wanted to see if the picture books in the library fairly represented the students served by the library on a daily basis. The article is full of statistics, including the fact that of 216 books 116 featured only white characters. Only 7 of the 216 featured African American main characters. The article carefully categorizes the 216 books and demonstrates that we are not doing a very good job of serving the students in our changing communities.

Livingston, Nancy, and Catherine Kurkitan. "Circles and Celebrations: Learning About Other Cultures Through Literature." *The Reading Teacher* (April 2005): 696–703.

    This article highlights titles that feature food, fashion, fiestas, folklore, and famous people, and, more importantly, literature, philosophy, social, economic, and political issues involved with diversity. Many titles are annotated and there is a section of information about author Pam Muñoz Ryan.

Louie, Belinda Y. "Guiding Principles for Teaching Multicultural Literature." *The Reading Teacher* (February 2006): 438–48.

    To help teachers select appropriate materials for teaching multicultural literature, the author of this article has developed some guiding principles. An example of these principles includes the following: check authenticity, understand the world of ethnic characters, see the world through the characters' perspectives, and identify values that shape conflict-resolution strategies.

Mathis, Janelle. "Respond to Stories with Stories: Teachers Discuss Multicultural Children's Literature." *The Social Studies* (July/August 2001): 155–60.

 It is important to provide many opportunities for discussion when reading multicultural literature. Recognize the power of stories to help children develop a sensitive perspective on diversity issues and to value literature describing other cultures and different experiences.

Mendoza, Jean, and Debbie Reese. "Examining Multicultural Picture Books for the Early Childhood Classroom: Possibilities and Pitfalls." *Early Childhood Research and Practice* (fall 2001). Available at http://ecrp.uiuc.edu/v3n2/mendoza.html

 It is important to introduce young children to diverse cultures using quality picture books. These books can serve as learning tools as well as a source of affirmations. However, not all picture books provide a realistic view. This article addresses authenticity and states that there is not enough criticism of titles available to help adults make good choices. Adults need to be aware that sharing one book is not enough to address the diversity issue; there simply are not enough accurate titles available today.

Meyer, Calvin F., and Elizabeth Kelley Rhoads. "Multiculturalism: Beyond Food, Festival, Folklore, and Fashion." *Kappa Delta Pi Record* (winter 2006): 82–87.

 This article includes many statistics about changing demographics in United States public schools and concludes that in 2020, minorities will comprise one-half of the students in our nation's public schools. We need to move away from the emphasis on food, festivals, folklore, and fashion, which emphasizes the differences; instead, we need to teach understanding, respect, and similarities and work hard to transform existing attitudes. The article also includes guidelines to selecting good multicultural literature for students.

Shorr, Pamela Wheaton. "Teaching America's Immigrants." *Instructor* (August 2006): 46–53.

 Some amazing statistics about the current foreign born population of the USA today are listed in the beginning of this article. It is important to give these students a place in the classroom and to provide them with the help they will need to be successful.

# Internet Resources

**Books written in two languages:** http://www.fpg.unc.edu/~nv/pages/res_books.cfm

**A World of Difference Institute: Recommended Multicultural and Anti-Bias Books for Children in Grades K–6:** http://www.adl.org/bibliography/

**Cynthia Leitich Smith:** http://www.cynthialeitichsmith.com/lit_resources/diversity/diversity.html

**Understanding Prejudice.org:** http://www.understandingprejudice.org/

**Reading Is Fundamental's List "100 of the Decade's Best Multicultural Read-Alouds":** http://www.rif.org/educators/books/100_best_multicultural.mspx

**Diversity Central (focuses on business statistics):** http://www.diversitycentral.com/

**Teaching Tolerance Magazine (free publication):** http://www.teachingtolerance.org

# Books That Include Other Languages

Ada, Alma Flor. *Gathering the Sun: An ABC in Spanish and English*. HarperCollins, 2001. ISBN 0-688-17067-6 Gr. K–3

Alarcon, Francisco X. *Poems to Dream Together/Poemas Para Sonar Juntos*. Lee & Low, 2005. ISBN 1-58430-233-X Gr. 3–5

_____. *Angels Ride Bikes Los Angeles Andan en Bicicleta: And Other Fall Poems*. Children's Book Press, 2005. ISBN 0-89239-198-7 Gr. PS–17

_____. *Iguanas in the Snow and Other Winter Poems*. Children's Book Press, 2004. ISBN 0-89239-168-5 Gr. K–5

Alvarez, Julia. *How Tia Lola Came to (Visit) Stay*. Knopf, 2001. ISBN 0-375-90215-5 Gr. 3–5

Ancona, George. *Mi Barrio: My Neighborhood*. Scholastic Library Publishing, 2005. ISBN 0-516-25064-7 Gr. 1–3

Bertrand, Diane Gonzales. *The Last Doll/La Ultima Muneca*. Arte Publico, 2001. ISBN 1-55885-290-7 Gr. 1–4

Cisneros, Sandra. *Hairs/Pelitos*. Random House, 1997. ISBN 0-679-89007-2 Gr. PS–3

Delacre, Lulu. *Arroz con Leche: Popular Songs and Rhymes from Latin America*. Scholastic, 1992. ISBN 0-590-41886-8 Gr. PS–3

Dorros, Arthur. *Radio Man/Don Radio: A Story in English and Spanish*. HarperCollins, 1997. ISBN 0-06-443482-6 Gr. K–3

Elya, Susan Middleton. *Bebe Goes Shopping*. Harcourt, 2006. ISBN 0-15-205426-X Gr. K–2

Guy, Ginger Foglesong. *Siesta*. Greenwillow, 2005. ISBN 0-060-56061-4 PS

Herrera, Juan Felipe. *Grandma and Me at the Flea/Los Meros Meros Remateros*. Children's Book Press, 2004. ISBN 0-89239-171-5 Gr. 2–4

_____. *The Upside Down Boy/El Niño de Cabeza*. Children's Book Press, 2000. ISBN 0-89239-217-7 Gr. 2–5

Lachtman, Ofelia Dumas. *Pepita Talks Twice/Pepita Habla Dos Veces*. Arte Publico/Pinata, 1995. ISBN 1-55885-077-5 Gr. K–3

Lainez, Rene Colato. *Playing Loteria/El Juego Do al Loteria*. Luna Rising, 2005. ISBN 0-87358-881-9 Gr. 2–4

Lomas Garza, Carmen. *Family Pictures/Cuadros de Familia*. Children's Book Press, 2005. ISBN 0-89239-206-1 Gr. 1–4

Medina, Jane. *My Name Is Jorge: On Both Sides of the River*. Boyds Mills, 2003. ISBN 1-56397-811-3 Gr. 2–4

_____. *The Dream on Blanca's Wall: Poems in English and Spanish*. Boyds Mills, 2004. ISBN 1-56397-740-0 Gr. 2–4

Morales, Yuyi. *Just a Minute: A Trickster Tale and Counting Book.* Chronicle, 2003. ISBN 0-8118-3758-0 Gr. PS–2

Orozco, Jose-Luis. *De Colores and Other Latin American Folk Songs for Children.* DIANE, 2004. Gr. 0–4

Park, Linda Sue, and Julia Durango. *Yum! Yuck! A Foldout Book of People Sounds.* Charlesbridge, 2005. ISBN 1-57091-659-4 Gr. PS–7

Perez, Amada Irma. *My Very Own Room/Mi Propio Cuartito.* Children's Book Press, 2000. ISBN 0-89239-164-2 Gr. 1–4

_____. *My Diary from Here to There/Mi Diario de Aqui Hasta Alla.* Children's Book Press, 2004. ISBN 0-89239-175-8 Gr. 2–5

Salinal, Bobbi. *The Three Pigs/Los Tres Credos: Nachos, Tito, and Miguel.* Pinata, 1998. ISBN 0-934-92505-4 Gr. 1–6

Soto, Gary. *My Little Car.* Putnam, 2006. ISBN 0399-23220-6. Gr. PS–2

# Magazines

The following magazines are indexed in a recent volume of *Children's Magazine Guide*. The annotations provide a brief description of each publication's contents and audience. We recommend all the magazines and strongly urge our readers to call or write to individual publishers to obtain a sample copy. *Note:* Subscription prices are per year and in U.S. dollars, including pricing information for Canada (C), Mexico (M), and other foreign countries. Subscription prices are subject to change and may not include applicable taxes, such as Canada's GST.

*The Children's Magazine Guide: A Subject Index to Children's Magazines and Web Sites* is published at the end of each month by Libraries Unlimited, 88 Post Road West, Westport, CT 06881. See http://www.childrensmag.com for subscription pricing and information. Thank you to Kristina Sheppard, Managing Editor, for allowing us to include the following list of magazines from the *Children's Magazine Guide*:

**AMERICAN GIRL**
8400 Fairway Place
Middleton, WI 53562
(800) 234-1278
www.americangirl.com
Stories, games, and projects for girls, along with advice on growing up, fitting in, and getting along.
Ages 8–12. 6 issues.
US $22.95; C $29.00

**BIOGRAPHY TODAY**
Omnigraphics, Inc.
P.O. Box 625
Holmes, PA 19043
(800) 234-1340
www.omnigraphics.com
Profiles ten contemporary newsmakers per issue from fields such as entertainment, literature, politics, and sports.
Ages 10–15. 3 issues annually.
US and foreign $60.00

**COBBLESTONE**
Carus Publishing Company
30 Grove St. Ste. C
Peterborough, NH 03458
(800) 821-0115
www.cobblestonepub.com
Themed issues focusing on American history.
Ages 9–14. 9 issues.
US $29.95; C/Foreign $41.95

**CRINKLES**
Libraries Unlimited
88 Post Road West
Westport, CT 06881
888/371-0152
www.crinkles.com
Magazine for children to stimulate curiosity about people, places, things, and events. Designed to build critical thinking and library media skills.
Ages 7–11. 6 issues.
US $30.00; C/Foreign $43.00

**CURRENT EVENTS**
Weekly Reader Corporation
3001 Cindel Dr.
Delran, NJ 08075
(800) 446-3355
www.weeklyreader.com/store
National and foreign news.
Ages 10–16. 25 issues.
US $34.48; Classroom orders $8.95

**FACES**
Cobblestone Publishing Company
30 Grove St. Ste. C
Peterborough, NH 03458
(800) 821-0115
www.cobblestonepub.com
Theme-oriented issues on geography and world cultures.
Ages 8–14. 9 issues.
US $29.95; C/Foreign $41.95

**GIRLS' LIFE**
Monarch Services, Inc.
4517 Harford Road
Baltimore, MD 21214
888/999-3222
www.girlslife.com
Packed with the best advice on dealing with friends, parents, school, siblings, popularity, best friends, and worst enemies. Plus, great features that reach into every part of a girl's life, including beauty, fashion, and boys.
Ages 10–15. 6 issues.
US $14.95; C $19.95; Other foreign $45.00

**JUNIOR SCHOLASTIC**
Scholastic Inc.
2931 E. McCarty St., P.O. Box 3710
Jefferson City, MO 65102-3710
(800) 724-6527
www.juniorscholastic.com
For price in Canada, contact:
Scholastic Canada Ltd.

175 Hillmount Rd.
Markham, ON L6C 1Z7
(800) 268-3860, www.scholastic.ca
U.S. and world affairs, current events, history, citizenship, and geography.
Ages 11–15. 18 issues.
US $12.75.

## KNOW YOUR WORLD EXTRA

Weekly Reader Corporation
3001 Cindel Dr.
Delran, NJ 08075
(800) 446-3355
www.weeklyreader.com/store
High-interest news articles, true-life adventures, and challenging activities.
Ages 11–17. 12 issues.
US $34.50; Classroom orders $10.50

## NATIONAL GEOGRAPHIC

National Geographic Society
P.O. Box 63001
Tampa, FL 33663-3001
(800) 647-5463
www.nationalgeographic.com
Articles, photographs and maps about people, places, and animals around the world.
Ages 12 and up. Monthly.
US $34.00; C $38.00; Other foreign $49.50

## NATIONAL GEOGRAPHIC KIDS

National Geographic Society
P.O. Box 63001
Tampa, FL 33663-3001
(800) 647-5463
www.nationalgeographic.com/ngkids
Wild animals, pets, science, outdoors, hobbies, and sports explored through articles, photographs, games, and posters.
Ages 6–12. 10 issues.
US $19.95; C $26.00; Other foreign $29.95

## NEW MOON

New Moon Publishing, Inc.
34 E. Superior St., #200
Duluth, MN 55802
(800) 381-4743
www.newmoon.org
Fiction, nonfiction, advice, and activities to encourage self-esteem in girls.
Ages 8–14. 6 issues
US $29.00; C $39.00; Other foreign $44.00

**SCHOLASTIC NEWS**
Scholastic Inc.
2931 E. McCarty St., P.O. Box 3710
Jefferson City, MO 65102-3710
(800) 724-6527
www.scholasticnews.com
For price in Canada, contact:
Scholastic Canada Ltd.
175 Hillmount Rd.
Markham, ON L6C 1Z7
(800) 268-3860, www.scholastic.ca
Current events newsweekly with timely stories and features.
*Scholastic News-4*, Ages 8–10
*Scholastic News-Sr*, Ages 10–12
24 issues.
US $4.90.

**TEEN NEWSWEEK**
Weekly Reader Corporation
3001 Cindel Dr.
Delran, NJ 08075
(800) 446-3355
www.weeklyreader.com/teens/newsweek
Covers news including politics, sports, and science through cover stories, debates, and work sheets.
Ages 11–14. 26 issues.
US $9.85

**TIME FOR KIDS**
Time Inc.
P.O. Box 60001
Tampa, FL 33660-0001
TFK-NS: (800) 950-5954
TFK-WR: (800) 777-8600
www.timeforkids.com
Weekly news magazine with high-interest, nonfiction articles and features.
*News Scoop Edition*, Ages 7–9
*World Report Edition*, Ages 9–12
26 issues.
US $24.95

**WEEKLY READER**
Weekly Reader Corporation
3001 Cindel Dr.
Delran, NJ 08075
(800) 446-3355
www.weeklyreader.com/store
Theme and news-based issues for high-interest nonfiction reading.
*Weekly Reader 4*, Ages 8–10.
*Weekly Reader Sr*, Ages 10–12.
25 issues.
US $24.95; Classroom orders $3.75

# Author Index

# Title Index

# About the Authors

LIZ KNOWLES, Ed.D., received her undergraduate degree in Elementary Education from Central Connecticut State University; a master's degree in Reading from Nova Southeastern University in Ft. Lauderdale, Florida; and an Ed.D. in Curriculum Development and Systemic Change, also from Nova Southeastern University. Liz has been an elementary teacher, grades K–6, for thirty years. She has also been an adjunct professor, teaching graduate courses in reading, at Florida Atlantic University. She currently serves as Director of Professional Development and Curriculum for both campuses (Ft. Lauderdale and Boca Raton) of Pine Crest School in Florida.

MARTHA SMITH received her undergraduate degree in Library Science from Eastern Michigan University and a master's degree of education in Library Science from the University of South Florida. Martha has been a media specialist for more than twenty years in the Pre-K through eighth-grade setting and is currently serving as Library Media Specialist at Pine Crest School, Boca Raton, Florida.